The Memoirs of a N

WET
AND
DRY

Commander Geoffrey Greenish

The Memoirs of a Naval Officer

WET AND DRY

Commander Geoffrey Greenish

BREWIN BOOKS

BREWIN BOOKS
56 Alcester Road,
Studley,
Warwickshire,
B80 7LG
www.brewinbooks.com

Published by Brewin Books 2011

A CIP catalogue record for this book is available
from the British Library.

ISBN: 978-1-85858-479-9

Printed by Hobbs the Printers Ltd.

CONTENTS

PREFACE

A T A LATE stage in life I have been persuaded to write my Memoirs and do so because I feel that the life my generation lived was so different to that of succeeding generations, that it contains interest and lessons for them.

I spent all 47 years of my working life from the age of 17 to 65 in the service of my country. This was divided into 35 years in the Royal Navy, the last 8 of which overlapped a further 12 years or 20 years in all, in the Defence Intelligence business. In effect, I had two almost separate careers and I can truthfully say that both were extremely varied, interesting and satisfying.

I was never well paid when working but now have adequate pensions, including a tax-free war disability pension. Today people tend to think and work entirely for themselves with money as the main motivation. Whilst they may be richer than my generation, they will not necessarily be happier. Vocation and service are more satisfying.

World War II is receding into history and Soviet Communism has collapsed. Now we have a more complex and fractious world where war has become endemic. Although we cannot forecast the future precisely, the lessons of history suggest that we lower our guard at our peril. We need to be able to defend ourselves against whatever threat materializes. Neglect of our defences caused many disasters in World War II and one hopes that this will never be forgotten.

These memoirs cover my professional career rather than my personal and family life, but there were times when the two became intertwined. On these occasions and where the family have influenced my career, they have been included. Indeed, the book is dedicated to my family, particularly the younger members. They and others may be interested in the life that my generation led, particularly in the years of World War II when I too was pretty young.

Robertsbridge, 2011

CHAPTER 1

SCHOOL DAYS

FROM ABOUT THE age of eight I developed a very strong desire to join the Royal Navy. Where this came from I do not know. My father, a GP, had served in the Royal Navy as a Surgeon Lieutenant from 1916-18 during World War I. Most of his service was in HMS "Royal Oak" a then modern battleship based at Scapa Flow. He joined after the Battle of Jutland and apart from the occasional sweep down the North Sea, the Grand Fleet spent most of its time at Scapa Flow. Our house was full of things, such as a brass electric kettle manufactured on board by the engine room staff who clearly had time on their hands. My father beat the Captain to win the wardroom billiards competition! He was never blessed with tact. Apart from another surgeon who served in the Navy in the 19th Century, my family had no other naval connections. However my father's family came from Pembrokeshire and a paternal Great Grandfather built the fishing docks at Milford Haven and owned a fleet of trawlers. My maternal Grandfather was a London Ship Broker and descended from a Scottish family of ship builders and owners at Kincardine in the Firth of Forth. So we certainly had connections with the sea and perhaps that is where my interest in the Navy stemmed from.

Like most middle class boys of those times, I was dispatched from home at Fleet in Hampshire, to a boarding preparatory school at the age of eight. Also typical of those times, my parents chose the school, Field Place, Highcliffe near Bournemouth as I had a Great Uncle and Aunt living in the village nearby. The quality of the school was not considered. This was unfortunate as it turned out to be a very poorly run school. During my five years there the school had four different Headmasters. When I joined the school in 1931 there were 60 boys, when I left there were 16! Initially there was considerable bullying. In full view of the Headmaster, the school bully spent our periods in the swimming pool ducking the smaller boys. There was no swimming instruction and as a result I am a poor self-taught swimmer. Incidentally the pool was always pea green and it was never treated with chemicals. It was also unheated. In retrospect I realised that the teaching was very varied, the masters were nearly all oddball bachelors who lived in a bungalow in the school grounds. Our French and Geography master was Sam Malins, who was just down from University and whose younger brother was in the Royal Navy. Captain Wickham Malins became one of the band of Destroyer Captains who did so well in the war and whom I eventually met when we were both retired. Sam Malins was lost when HMS "Dunedin" was torpedoed and sunk in the south Atlantic. Another Master was Lieutenant Commander Axten, who taught maths and who had left the Navy under the 'Geddes' axe after World War I. He once took two of us to Portsmouth to have tea in the old Royal Yacht "Victoria and Albert" where the navigator was an old friend of his.

But boys will be boys and we had plenty of fun. We were divided into Trojans and Spartans and spent much of our spare time building bunkers and dugouts and fighting mock battles. Another activity was visiting neighbouring dormitories at night by climbing out of the windows and creeping along a narrow ledge outside - a miracle nobody fell and got injured. In those days there were no half terms and one's parents appeared once a year for sports day in the summer. Whilst I was no athlete, I did enjoy the soccer and cricket we played and matches against neighbouring schools. My Great Uncle and Aunt would occasionally have me out for Sunday lunch and I was always returned to school with a large bar of Bournville chocolate, which was a welcome addition to the sixpence a week we were allowed to spend at the tuck shop. During my prep school days, I built up a large collection of Dinky toy warships, a complete fleet of battleships, cruisers and destroyers organized in squadrons and flotillas, the details of which I got from Oscar Parkes "All the World's Navies". In carpentry lessons I made book cases etc, and docks for my ships. In my last year, my fourth Headmaster, Mr Davidson, invited me to sail in his 5 ton yawl from the Hamble River to Christchurch, where I first experienced sea sickness. He also owned a 1929 3 litre Bentley Tourer which was big enough to take the entire soccer or cricket team to away matches. He was in the RAF VR and sadly was killed in a flying accident in 1939.

In the spring of 1936, at the age of 13, I went to London to attend the interview, medical and exams for entry into Dartmouth. Much to the consternation of my father, I failed. On enquiring from the Admiralty, he was told I had failed Latin and French. In view of the sort of school I was at this was not altogether surprising. In retrospect it turned out to be a major blessing for me and the first of many slices of luck that seemed to have accompanied me throughout my life. After unsuccessful attempts to get me into Epsom or Charterhouse, my father sent me to Cheltenham College, his old school. I arrived for the summer term of 1936 and unusually, took the Common Entrance Exam on the first day of term. As a result I did not do well and started in the bottom form. On the plus side, I had the good fortune to join what was undoubtedly the best of the six boarding houses at college, Christowe. My Housemaster, Mr King, was a bachelor who had been severely wounded in World War I. He was a Martinet, a strict disciplinarian who ran a taught ship but who had a heart of gold. He used to go to the farms in the Cotswolds and bring back such delicacies as asparagus and strawberries for his 60 boys and we were recognized as the best fed House in the College. He also chose a good team of House Prefects whom the younger boys could look up to and respect. There was never any bullying nor drug or drink problems. Mr King was pretty free with the cane and for various reasons which would now be regarded as trivial, I was caned four times by him during my early years. In the summer term, boys could either row or play cricket. However the number who could row was limited and unless you were useless at it, you played cricket. I eventually reached the house first teams for rugby, cricket and hockey but never reached college teams. In 1937 I took up fencing and found that I had a talent for it, aided by being left handed. I was taught by the senior PT instructor, a retired Army RSM and I enjoyed fencing matches against other public schools. In 1939 I was runner up in the Public Schools Junior Foil Championship. The following year three of us, "Body" Hosking, Graham Jackson and I won the Public School Championship. Hosking was the sabre champion and the three of us accrued enough points in the final pools of all three weapons – foil, sabre and epée – to win the Gold Challenge Cup. Interestingly, both Hosking and Jackson became rugby internationals after the war, playing for England and Scotland respectively.

Although it was voluntary, all boys without exception joined the Officers Training Corps (OTC) on reaching 15, prior to which one joined the boy scouts. One turned out in World War I style khaki uniforms once a week and once a term we had a field day out in the Cotswold countryside. This was a break from school and great fun. Its more serious purpose was to teach the elements of field tactics and led, after about 2 years, to the taking of an exam called "Cert A", which also included map reading. At the end of the field day we would march back to college led by the college band in which, for a term or two, I played the big drum.

After "Cert A" OTC life got more interesting. I did a term in the machine gun section learning about the new Bren gun with which we had just been issued. In my final terms I joined the signal section and learned Morse, Heliograph signaling, flag signaling and radio. We had two old wireless sets, originally designed to be carried by mules. On field days, these would be taken out by truck (no mules at Cheltenham College) and set up and operated several miles apart. My knowledge of communications proved very valuable later in the Navy. In the summer of, I think, 1938 I went to the OTC camp at Bisley where we met units from other schools and fired live rounds from our .303 rifles and Bren guns on the famous ranges.

Another enjoyable activity at Cheltenham was our expeditions into the Cotswolds on Sundays. Although the town was out of bounds we were allowed, after morning chapel, to take our bicycles with a picnic lunch and ride into the country. The bag lunch was augmented by bangers and beans bought at the tuck shop and cooked on a wood fire in the woods. The afternoon would end with a hair raising ride down the steep hills into Cheltenham, in time to change back into our Sunday black suits for the evening chapel service (twice on Sundays and daily during the week). At this point I might mention that my school holidays were usually spent at home at Fleet except that every summer, my father took a month off. In my younger days we would make the long drive to Broad Haven in Pembrokeshire where my parents rented a house near the beach. My father was born at Haverfordwest where my Grandfather had been a JP, High sheriff for a year, a Doctor of Music and organist of the Parish Church as well as part owner of a large department store. A curious mixture, which did however mean that the family was well known. We are also hereditary Freeman of the town descending from a Philip Greenish who was made a Freeman in 1734 for reasons which we have never been able to discover. In those days, the enormous beach at Broad Haven in St Brides Bay was virtually deserted and idyllic days were spent flying kites, boating, playing cricket and swimming. Fresh bread was obtainable at Little Haven a mile away, lobsters in baskets by the roadside and occasionally, the family would go prawn fishing at Sandy Haven near Milford Haven.

On the scholastic side at Cheltenham, because of my poor Common Entrance results, I started in the bottom form. However in each of the next two terms I was moved up a year from the 2nd to the 4th Division winning a couple of form prizes on the way. Now at my proper level I took "School Certificate" at 16 and a year later in 1940, the Special Entry Navy Exam. Meanwhile World War II had started and Cheltenham College was requisitioned by the Government.

When war was declared on Germany by Great Britain on 3rd September 1939 the family was travelling home to Fleet from a caravan holiday at Little Common near Bexhill, and we stopped to listen on the radio to Chamberlain's famous broadcast. The remainder of that summer holiday was spent digging an air raid shelter in the garden at Fleet. I had taken my School Certificate exams (equivalent to "O" Levels) that summer, but before returning to Cheltenham for the winter term, we were suddenly told that the Government had requisitioned the College and we were to be transferred to Shrewsbury School. It was rumoured that if London had to be evacuated, "Big Class" (the College Assembly Room) or the Chapel at Cheltenham was to become a temporary House of Commons because of their similar configuration with seats facing each other. At Shrewsbury we were billeted around the town and shared the school facilities with Shrewsbury boys – we played games in the morning and attended school in the afternoon, Shrewsbury vice versa. Four of us from Christowe were billeted about four miles out of town with a charming elderly couple, who fed us, and where we shared a large bedroom. We all had bicycles which we used to travel to Shrewsbury and back and one of my abiding memories of that time is catching the huge sugar beet lorries which travelled daily into Shrewsbury and virtually free riding in their slipstream into Shrewsbury, watching carefully to miss any beets that fell off the back! I also recall a long remembered college rugby match against Rugby which was only settled in the last minutes by an incredible drop goal by "Body" Hosking from the half way line. Shrewsbury was a soccer school and they were deeply impressed! We spent two terms at Shrewsbury during a very cold and snowy winter but, after the phoney war, returned to Cheltenham for the summer term in 1940. Here, we suddenly found we had a centralised Dining Hall and catering in the old library (as opposed to meals at Christowe). We also had a new Headmaster, Mr Elliott-Smith (my fourth whilst at college) who immediately became unpopular by abolishing House "Pots" (inter-house games competitions). I had become a House Prefect but my main occupation was final preparations for the Navy Exam, including a crash course in European and American history (I had decided to take Modern History as my main subject). The Civil Service Commissioners Special Entry Exam normally covered entry into Sandhurst, Woolwich, Cranwell and the Navy, but all but the Navy had closed their regular officer entry for the duration of the war and competition for the 15 places in the RN Executive Branch was expected to be severe, so on this, my first attempt at the age of 17, I was not expected to succeed. After the interview and medical in London and the exams at Cheltenham, I think in July 1940, we were then sent, for the remainder of the term, to the Forest of Dean to assist in forestry work. At the end of the term, most of Christowe went to a Cotswolds farm to help with the harvest (bearing in mind that men were being called up for war service). It was while there that a telegram was received from home to say I had passed into the Royal Navy and would I please come home at once! I got the 14th place and Tony Scott-Langley, also from Christowe, got 15th. Body Hosking passed into the Royal Marines but the other four candidates from Cheltenham all, alas, failed to get a place. My Housemaster, Mr King, who was at the farm, was astonished and I later heard that I was destined to be Head of House as other senior boys were leaving in droves to join up. It is sad to relate that friendships established at college did not last as we all went our separate ways and with few exceptions, never saw each other again. In due course I saw the marks for the Navy exam. I had record History marks, which were entirely responsible for getting me through. I was only home for about a fortnight, during which two visits were paid to Gieves the Naval Tailors in London to be measured and fitted with uniforms, both blues and whites (for tropical wear) and including a white pith helmet which was still required and kept in a special tin case, though I never ever wore it!

CHAPTER 2

ENTRY INTO THE ROYAL NAVY

IN LATE AUGUST 1940, still only 17, it was off to Dartmouth for a special four months cadets training as the Training Cruiser, to which Special Entry Cadets normally went, had long since gone to war. Bear in mind that through the spring and summer of 1940 the war had suddenly taken off: Norway, the Low Countries and France had all fallen and the Battle of Britain was just starting. So the atmosphere at Dartmouth, as elsewhere, was one of crisis and training was interspersed with digging trenches and preparing for invasion. At Dartmouth, the 15 Executive Cadets were joined by RN Engineer and Paymaster Cadets, a large contingent of Canadians, several cadets from the Indian Navy, some Australians, a South African and latterly, some Free French cadets – over 80 in all. The Officers on the staff were a mixed lot of retired and active service, as were the Chiefs and Petty Officers. We slept in hammocks and our days were a mixture of Parade Ground Drill and instruction in Seamanship, Signals and Navigation to name a few subjects – long, hard days doubling between classes and little spare time. At our first parade, I well remember the Petty Officer asking who had been NCOs in the OTC and surprisingly I was one of the very few (I had been a sergeant in the Cheltenham College OTC) so was immediately called out to be the leading Cadet for the day – thus learning the age old naval tradition – never volunteer! Other memories of an incredibly busy four months include capsizing a dinghy in the River Dart in November with Tony Langley, spending a long cold hour or more in the water and losing any enthusiasm for dinghy sailing! On Saturday evenings we were given shore leave for a few hours and spent our hard earned one shilling a day pay learning, from our older Canadian and French colleagues, how to drink beer at the local pub! I also played rugger for the

'Frobisher' team and won the Cadets fencing competition which earned me two silver napkins. At the end of four months in December 1940, we sat exams and I surprisingly won a book prize (the Eardley Howard Crockett Prize) which I still have, as runner up to the Engineer cadet who won the King's Dirk. Home for Christmas leave and to await appointments to our first ships. Mine was to the new battleship "Prince of Wales" but a week later, was superseded by another to the 25 year old 'D' class Cruiser "Danae" in the Far East! I never discovered why this change was made but it was another fortuitous event which turned out to be very lucky for me. Had I gone to the "Prince of Wales" I might well have been killed during her action with the "Bismark" (one of my term was killed), certainly sunk by the Japanese in December 1941 and either killed or taken prisoner when "Exeter" was sunk leaving the Java sea battle, as all the Midshipmen from "Prince of Wales" had been transferred to her.

In January 1941 I joined the troopship "Orontes" at Glasgow for passage to Halifax, Nova Scotia en route to the Far East. In "Orontes" I joined 17 other midshipmen and a draft of about 400 ratings destined for "Danae", "Durban" and "Dauntless". There were also some Canadian midshipmen returning to Canada for leave. Amongst these was Bill Howe whose father was the Canadian Minister of Transport. When we reached Halifax after our convoy across the Atlantic and boarded our special train, we found crates of liquor and other delights – the gift of Mr C D Howe! First reactions to Canada were the bright lights everywhere, so startling after the black out in wartime Britain and, of course, the snow which was with us all the way to Vancouver. Our train journey took 5 days, with one 20 minute stop and one 10 minute stop each day. Porters lowered and made up the bunks each night. The food, after wartime Britain, was fabulous. From Vancouver we were ferried to Victoria BC on Vancouver Island, where we were billeted for two weeks in the Quarantine Station. Memories of Victoria are vague except for attending a ball at the Empress Hotel with girlfriends provided. We also hired a self-drive car and drove to Nanaimo, where we skated on an indoor rink. Our journey onwards was in the New Zealand shipping Company liner "Aorangi" on her normal peacetime run from Vancouver to Fiji, then Auckland and finally Sydney. A long passage across the Pacific during which we kept watches on the bridge to keep us occupied and to learn some navigation. At Sydney we were again billeted in the Quarantine Station for a few days before sailing in a small Burns Phillips Coaster up the Australian coast via Brisbane, Cairns and Darwin, then to Surabaya, Semarang and Batavia in what was then the Dutch East Indies and finally Singapore. Here we learned that "Danae" was at Penang and so those midshipmen and ratings destined for her took an overnight train via Kuala Lumpur. The train incidentally was air conditioned, my first encounter with what was then a rare thing.

CHAPTER 3

TO WAR IN MY FIRST SHIP

O N 16TH APRIL 1941 after a journey lasting nearly three months I finally arrived on board my first ship, a 24 year old 4,000 ton light cruiser with 6 hand loaded 6-inch guns, 12 torpedo tubes and 3 antiquated 4-inch AA guns. Here, we were destined to do our Midshipman's training, shortened from 2½ years to 20 months because of the war. The six Midshipmen lived with three Sub Lieutenants in the Gunroom, a compartment about 15x12 feet with just room for a table, sideboard, long settee and two armchairs. Here we lived, had our meals and did our paperwork. Next door was the chest flat with just room for six chests. The Sub Lieutenants had cabins; we slept on portable camp beds, usually on the Quarterdeck because hammocks were far too hot in a tropical climate. One of the Sub Lieutenants was Anthony Frodsham, an Engineer who, many years later became the Secretary General of the Engineering Employers Federation. An ebullient character who enlivened life in the Gunroom and who later became a close friend when we both had apartments in Antibes in France.

Occasionally the Gunroom dined formally and any alleged misdemeanor would lead to the President ordering 'scuttle drill'. The culprit would be pushed through the scuttle (port hole) into the sea and would then have to swim to the gangway and climb up the quarterdeck. "Danae" was an old ship and having spent years in the tropics was alive with cockroaches. After a night watch, we used to visit the Gunroom for a drink of lime juice before turning in. As one switched on the lights the whole compartment was alive with hundreds of cockroaches running for cover and in seconds they had all disappeared. However, one was aware that they were never far away.

In World War I Penang had been attacked by the German Cruiser "Emden" and, to avoid a repetition, the three cruisers each did six week spells anchored as Guard Ship. Interspersed with this, we frequently escorted cargo/liners to and from Colombo. At sea, we were in three watches on the bridge, while in harbour, when not under instruction, two midshipmen ran the two ships' boats and the other four kept watches on the Quarterdeck. In October 1941 "Danae" went into dry dock at the Singapore naval base for a six week refit and the whole ship's company moved to the Fleet Shore Accommodation (FSA) just outside the dockyard. This was modern, comfortable, newly built accommodation with a swimming pool and sports grounds and so was paradise after our cramped ship. In November 1941, "Danae" paid visits to Cavite, the US Naval base near Manila in the Philippines and then Hong Kong, where we went into blue uniform for the only time I was in "Danae". On this visit, our Gunroom Leading Steward, Ah Lim, got married in Wanchei and some of the Gunroom Officers attended. I might mention at this point that a Midshipman's pay was 5 shillings (25p) a day or £7.50 a month from which about £5 went to pay one's mess bill, leaving £2.50 for everything else, including a run ashore! In Singapore, where the city was about 20 miles from the naval base, this meant once a month if that. But this period of comparative peace was coming to an end. Returning to Singapore we found that the battleships "Prince of Wales" and "Repulse" had arrived with their four attendant destroyers and had taken our accustomed berth. However on 6th December we left for Colombo and then to "Trincomali" the naval base on the East Coast of Ceylon. On the very next day after our departure, on 7th December, the Japanese attacked Pearl Harbour and Malaysia and the news soon became ominous. We were ordered back to Singapore but, by the time we got there, the great ships had been sunk and, apart from the destroyers, the naval base was ours again. There was a great sense of shock and impending disaster as Japanese troops were already advancing south from their landings in North East Malaysia. For the next six weeks, we were employed escorting troop convoys to Singapore, picking them up in the Indian Ocean and then through the Sunda and Banka Straits. Initially we met no trouble, but as the Japanese got closer to Singapore things started getting nasty and we were regularly bombed by large formations of bombers, as we approached Singapore. On a brief visit to the naval base on the north side of the island, we became aware of a sense of bitterness because the white civilian population were continuing their gay and frivolous lives in Singapore as if nothing was happening. As our last and largest troop convoy approached Singapore on 5th February 1942, we were heavily bombed by formations of 27 bombers and strafed by fighters. We were stuck in the swept Channel with paravanes out (an old fashioned protection from mines) doing 10 knots and unable to manoeuvre. At this point, I should say that our old 6-inch guns were only good for surface targets and our 4-inch AA guns, with no fire control, virtually useless. We suffered many near misses and the ship was plastered with bullets from Japanese fighter aircraft, many of which we later picked out of the superstructure. Miraculously we survived and our only casualty was the Captain's Secretary who I distinctly remember being carried down from the bridge covered in blood and looking very shocked, but the bullet had only grazed his chest and he was OK! Not so the "Empress of Asia", the biggest troopship, which was hit and caught fire. One of our midshipmen was sent over with the motor cutter to join other small craft rescuing thousands of troops, who were landed in the clothes they stood up in and nothing else. A week or so later Singapore fell and they all became prisoners of war. Meanwhile we went alongside in Keppel Harbour the commercial port. Ahead and astern of us were ships who had discharged their cargoes and were now embarking white women and children who were being evacuated. In the warehouses or godowns as they were known locally, were drunken Australian soldiers looting what they could find. A pall of smoke hung over the doomed city and Japanese bombers appeared from time to time. On 7th February we departed for the last time and though bombed on the way down, safely reached Tanjong Priok, the port for Batavia (now Djakarta) in the Dutch East Indies. Singapore surrendered to the Japanese soon after, on 15th February 1942.

For the next two weeks we were based at Tanjong Priok and unlike the British civilians in Singapore who took no interest in us, the Dutch were extremely hospitable. I recall dining at the Harmony Club in Batavia with two other Midshipmen as the guests of the Dutch manager of one of the local breweries, together with his daughter and two other charming teenage girls. One of them whom subsequently married one of the Midshipmen, Dick Fisher, after the war and after she had spent over 3 years in a Japanese internment camp. Operationally, we carried out sweeps with the Dutch cruisers stationed in Java and also went to Padang, in southern Sumatra, to rescue hundreds of British troops who had escaped from Singapore by boat and then walked across Sumatra. We took them to Tjilachap on the south coast of Java where we ran aground. It was an extremely hot afternoon and extremely worrying, as we thought we were stuck for good at the mercy of the Japanese bombers. With the aid of a small tug we eventually got free and returned to Tanjong Priok.

Towards the end of February 1942, it became apparent that a Japanese invasion of the Dutch East Indies was expected, but from which Strait to the North was uncertain. The stronger force of the Dutch cruisers "Java" and "de Reuter", the British cruiser "Exeter", Australian "Perth" and US "Houston" was based at Surabaya to defend the Makasser Straits. "Danae" with her sister ship "Dragon" and the Australian cruiser "Hobart" with two old destroyers remained at Tanjong Priok to defend the Banka Strait. Because of our weak air defence our squadron carried out two night sweeps northwards towards the Banka Strait expecting to meet Japanese forces advancing to invade Java and Sumatra. My action station was in the Fire Control Station (TS) in the bowels of the ship where, with headphones, I was in touch with the Gunnery Officer high up in the Spotting Top and applied his orders on to our ancient Fire Control Table. Bear in mind that we had no radar and depended on human eyesight aided by binoculars and optical range finders. I well remember those night sweeps, knowing that if we met the Japanese, the action would be brief and violent, our torpedoes might do damage but we stood little chance of surviving. In the event nothing happened and after the second sweep we had then been ordered to leave and withdraw to Colombo. This brave and sensible order was given by Commodore Collins RAN, the Allied Naval Chief of Staff. It prevented further useless loss of ships and nearly 1500 officers and men lived to fight another day. An hour after we cleared the Sunda Strait, an Indian Navy Frigate, with good AA, reported being bombed as she too escaped. Later it became clear that the Japanese force facing us had turned back for a few hours which explains why we missed them. However, the other Japanese force advancing down the Makasser Strait met the larger allied force and destroyed it in the Battle of the Java Sea. "Exeter" and "Perth" both damaged, tried to escape through the Sunda Strait but were caught and sunk by the Japanese forces that we had missed only a few hours after we passed through. As mentioned earlier, some term mates of mine, who had originally been in the "Prince of Wales" and survived her sinking, had been transferred to "Exeter" and were either killed or taken prisoner. It was, at this point, that I realised how incredibly lucky "Danae" had been and for the rest of the war, I had a strong feeling that I would survive. After another call at Padang for more Singapore survivors, we reached Colombo on 5th March 1942. My father later told me that one of his patients, a Royal Navy Captain working in the Admiralty had told him that our squadron was missing from the time of the Java Sea battle until our arrival at Colombo. Because ships kept radio silence at sea, no one knew whether we had been destroyed like the rest of the Allied Fleet or had survived. It is curious too, that as far as I know, no naval history covering the Java Sea battle mentions our existence.

A weary "Danae" stayed in Colombo for about 10 days for re-provisioning and repairs. The six Midshipmen were sent on a brief leave, in two batches of three, to a rubber plantation in southern Ceylon (Sri Lanka), where we were looked after by a Mr and Mrs Besant and where one got a feel of what their lives were like. On 18th March 1942 "Danae" left Colombo for Bombay and then proceeded to the Persian Gulf where we were to act as a Guard ship to protect the Gulf and the oil installations from Japanese attack. We first visited the oil refinery at Abadan, up the Shatt Al Arab river, where I recall a great welcome and an ENSA show by the British community. Twenty-four hours later, we moved to Basra and then down the Gulf visiting Bahrain and the desert town of Awali before spending a solid six weeks anchored at Khor Kuwai or patrolling the Straits of Hormuz. Very dull but essential for the Midshipmen, as a few weeks later, we took our Seamanship and Navigation exams. Apart from these main subjects, we had also done a month's Engine room training, a course in ship construction and lectures in other subjects related to naval life. While much of the engineering training was theoretical, we did do watches in the engine and boiler rooms, which in the tropics were unbelievably hot. The only relief was visiting the cold room during rounds of the outside machinery and drinking iced water. The old ship suffered severely from 'condenseritis' when tubes would spring a leak and allow sea water into the fresh water side. These leaks led to 'Canterbury tests' with which we became very familiar and which consisted basically of opening up and plugging the defective tubes. Normally, Midshipmen attended a fleet board for these exams but in our situation this was impossible. An "own ship" exam was rare and, of course, the ship's officers had to avoid any accusation of favouring their own Midshipmen. Our Navigation exam took place on 1st May while we were at sea and at Khor Kuwai while Seamanship Oral exams started on 6th May at Bahrain then at Lengen and back at Khor Kuwai. Not very good conditions for taking vital exams and I got 2nd classes for both Navigation and Seamanship. Among the other five Midshipmen, there was one other 2nd, two with 3rds, and two failures who had to re-sit. A further complication was the fact that our Captain, F J Butler, had suffered a nervous breakdown and was relieved during our exams by Captain Slattery (later Rear Admiral Sir Matthew Slattery, Chairman of BOAC), who had lost his cruiser in the Mediterranean - a distinguished man of whom we were much in awe. He was a very early Fleet Air Arm pilot (ex RNAS) and later I remember him giving us a fascinating talk about naval flying. On 14th May soon after our exams, "Danae" was relieved and went south to Mombasa. We met a heavy swell and I remember feeling seasick for the first time in "Danae". In earlier times "Danae" always seemed to be in a flat tropical calm. We arrived in Mombasa on 22nd May 1942 and were staggered to find a huge fleet in the Kilindini anchorage – 4 old 'R' class battleships, 3 Aircraft Carriers, cruisers and destroyers. However, we were due to leave for home and on 1st June four of the Midshipmen sailed in an elderly cargo liner for Britain. In those days, ships capable of 15 knots or more sailed independently and as our ship just qualified, we had a lonely voyage around the Cape, stopping briefly at Durban and Capetown and up past Freetown. We arrived safely in Britain on 14th July 1942 and not until after the war did I realize how lucky we had been again, because we came through the western approaches unescorted during the worst of the U-boat onslaught on our shipping. Of my 20 months as a Midshipman, I had been travelling for over 4 months! During my leave, I revisited Cheltenham College and saw all of my old Masters, which gave me the opportunity to thank them for getting me through the Navy exam.

I had now been in the navy for two years, had circumnavigated the world and was 19 years of age. After leave, all the surviving executive Midshipmen of my term both Dartmouth, Public School and ex lower deck entries, were promoted to acting Sub Lieutenants and on 23rd August 1942 started our technical courses. In peacetime these lasted 18 months but were now condensed to 4 months only. We were divided into groups and circulated around the technical schools, mostly in the Portsmouth area, for gunnery, torpedo, anti-submarine, signals and navigation etc, for 3 weeks in each and ending with an exam, the results of which affected one's seniority as a Lieutenant. I had only achieved 2nd classes for my seamanship and navigation in "Danae" (the own ship problem) but managed some 1st class passes for the technical courses. As a result I later got back-dated seniority as a confirmed Sub-Lieutenant and was promoted to Lieutenant on 1st August 1943 while I was still 20. During these courses, a Canadian term mate was killed by a German fighter bomber attack at the temporary torpedo school at Roedean School, Brighton (lovely notice in the dormitories inviting pupils to ring for a mistress if required!). The old Torpedo School, HMS "Vernon", had been destroyed by the German bombing of Portsmouth.

During our courses, our futures were being planned by the Appointers and we were informed that 50% of us would go to Submarines and 40% to Combined Ops (where our experience in boat handling as Midshipmen was needed in the rapidly expanding fleet of landing craft). I had wanted to join the Royal Navy from the age of about 8 and had developed a passionate desire to serve in destroyers so made this known on the preference form. I later asked to see our Appointer, Commander Deneys in London. After a chat with him, he said "Oh well I had better send you to my old ship". Thus it was that in January 1943 I joined the 'V' class Destroyer "Vanoc" in Gibraltar. Under the command of Deneys, she had, some months earlier, sunk the U-boat commanded by the ace Kretschmer and taken him prisoner. Only a handful of us went to destroyers, Henry Leach (later Admiral and First Sea Lord) went to a battleship and many were drafted, like it or not, into either combined Operations or Submarines, in which incidentally all the term's remaining war casualties occurred.

CHAPTER 4

DESTROYER TIME

S O I WAS fortunate once again and though "Vanoc" was also 25 years old like "Danae", she had modern asdics (Sonar) and radar. I was made Gunnery Control Officer and joined a very happy Wardroom of about 8 officers. The Captain was a Senior Commander named Churchill, but known universally as 'Bear's Breath Churchill' for obvious reasons. I shared a cabin with a RNVR Sub Lieutenant and it was entered through a manhole on the iron deck close to the Engine Room and down a vertical ladder. "Vanoc" being only 1200 tons and long and thin, was extremely lively at sea and our cabin was usually flooded with several inches of sea water, so you did not take your sea boots off until you got into your bunk! I was also extremely seasick but our First Lieutenant, 'Ginger' Cartwright, believed that a tot of neat rum before lunch would sufficiently paralyse the stomach to allow it to accept the disgusting tinned steak and kidney pudding or whatever else the Wardroom Chef could produce at sea. Gradually either the rum or experience began to tell, lunch stayed down longer and longer and I was never seasick again except on one occasion, which I shall come to later. I first learned to play liar dice in that Wardroom and all the old unmentionable songs that enlivened life in the Navy before TV etc. Drinking was pretty heavy in harbour although absolutely taboo at sea (except curiously for *that* rum). "Vanoc" belonged to the 13th Destroyer Flotilla based at Gibraltar. A mixed collection of old 'V' and 'W' class and modern "Hunt" class destroyers. The invasion of North Africa (Operation Torch) having taken place the previous November, our job was to escort convoys along the North African Coast to Oran, Algiers and as far as Bone. The German Air Force and U-boats were, at that time resisting strongly and we were frequently attacked by JU-88's. One of our 20mm AA guns was operated by a crack shot who shot down at least one. Even in harbour, life was violent – I remember once we were alongside in Bone with ammunition ships discharging around us when a stick of bombs exploded right down the centre of the basin. Had one of the ammunition ships been hit, we would hardly have survived. In Algiers one morning, an RAF Boston Bomber was shot down above the harbour (and above the clouds). We were suddenly aware of the plane screaming down and crashing barely 20 yards off our stern. Strong drinks after that! By way of relief, we were occasionally ordered South West from Gibraltar to escort ships coming from America via Casablanca. No air threat and we never encountered a U-boat. An overcrowded Gibraltar was desperately short of eggs in those days and Casablanca had plenty, so this trip was known as "The Egg Run". Large quantities of eggs were loaded all over the ship and even in the magazines and on the return run we just prayed we would not have to drop any depth charges, the explosions of which would have broken the lot! Sadly, life in "Vanoc" was not to last long, which was annoying as I had to get my watch keeping certificate before promotion to Lieutenant and one's Captain naturally would not award it until he was satisfied that by knowledge and experience, you could take charge of the ship at sea as Officer of the Watch. Sometime in March we were subjected to a heavy air attack at sea near Bone and 'near misses' were so close that the resultant shock to the old ship damaged our main engines. Standing on the bridge, one could see the bombs coming down and feel the ship shudder as they exploded, sometimes just feet away from the ship's side. We got back to Gibraltar where it was decided that "Vanoc" would return to Britain, pay off and the opportunity of repairs would be taken to convert her to a long range escort. This was being done to all the V and W's as opportunity offered – a boiler was removed and replaced with extra fuel tanks – maximum speed reduced from 35 to about 25 knots but range increased enormously and they became known as 'long leggers'. Returning to Britain we were one of the escorts of a large convoy which became shadowed by a large German Focke Wulf aircraft. It flew round and round the convoy outside normal gun range until eventually the Captain invited me to experiment with one of our surface action 4-inch guns and extra long timed fused shells. This was fun but as the gun trained round to follow the aircraft, it reached dead ahead. Now the old destroyers had foremasts which were supported by fore and aft wire stays. Suddenly, when the gun fired, there was an appalling crash and the heavy forestay fell across our open bridge. Fortunately no-one was injured and we all had a good laugh! Finally as the convoy moved up the west coast of Britain, we broke off and made for Falmouth as we were desperately short of fuel. We finally got alongside with 9 tons of fuel remaining – it might sound a lot but it amounts in fact, to the sludge in the bottom of the tanks.

Later we moved to Thorneycroft's at Southampton and paid off. On 24th April I left the ship and returned home to Fleet to await my next appointment. However on 1st May I was directed to proceed, post haste, to Devonport to join the "Hunt" class destroyer "Goathland" on a temporary appointment as Navigating Officer. "Goathland" had been hit during an action with 'E' boats in the channel and the First Lieutenant and Navigator were wounded, though not seriously. The "Hunt" class escort destroyers had been appearing in large numbers since 1940 – about 1200 tons and apart from the usual anti-submarine armament, had four or six 4-inch LA/AA dual purpose guns and a speed of 25 knots; very useful little ships. "Goathland" also had a notable Captain, Lieutenant Commander Nigel Pumphrey, who had already been awarded a DSO and a DSC from his time with coastal forces (MTB's and MGB's). The temporary First Lieutenant was Roddy MacDonald (later Vice Admiral Sir Roderick). The operational function of the "Hunt" flotilla at Devonport was to escort coastal convoys between Milford Haven, Plymouth and Portsmouth. Another flotilla at Portsmouth had a similar function. Because of the 'E' boat threat from French bases, convoys were sent into the safety of port at night, while the destroyers then went out as a fighting force to search for and do battle with the 'E' boats. The 'E' boats not only came over to attack any ships they could find, but also to lay mines. Round the British coasts were swept channels, kept clear by minesweepers but this took time and the swept channels were constantly being changed to avoid the latest mine lay. These changes were promulgated daily, almost hourly, by signal and one of my memories of six weeks in "Goathland" was the hours of work in the Charthouse keeping our charts corrected. By day, we had an easy time in fine weather escorting small coasters and the Captain slept and left us to it. By night, however, like a cat the Captain would surface and 3 or 4 "Hunts" would set off for the night's operation. By early 1943, Plymouth had powerful radar and VHF and HF voice radio and 'E' boat movements would be detected and reported. Our force would proceed to intercept but the situation was sometimes complicated by the presence of our own MGB's or MTB's also after 'E' boats, but not under our control. We also had a special radio operator who understood German and who operated special radio equipment (known as "Headache") in a little compartment on the bridge to intercept 'E' boat communications. As Navigator, my job was to ensure that our position was known at all times. The electric plotting table, which was inconveniently situated in the wheelhouse, was found to be incapable of keeping pace with rapid and continuous course changes so I spent my time at the chart table on the bridge under a canvas cover, hand plotting our movements and those of the 'E' boats who were also of course moving at high speed. These chases might last several hours and be punctuated by violent action at fairly close range with our 4-inch and two pounder guns firing and the 'E' boats fire coming at us. They had a tendency to fire over us and we often saw tracer coming straight for us and then, at the last minute, going over. On one night, a force of 4 "Hunts" split up and the following morning "Wensley-dale" appeared in Plymouth with a large hole in her side made, it transpired, by a British 4-inch shell! This was probably fired by "Krakoviak" a Polish manned "Hunt", whose fierce hatred of Germans caused them to be regarded as dangerous companions, since they tended to fire first and identify afterwards! One afternoon, while escorting a convoy to Plymouth, we got a good asdic contact and, unsure if it was sub or non-sub, dropped one depth charge. It was a huge shoal of white fish and dozens surfaced in a stunned state. We risked stopping in the shoal, lowered the whaler and recovered as many fish as we could. Far too much for us, so on arrival in Devonport that evening, a truck full of fish was sent to Plymouth hospital – manna from heaven in wartime.

After my six weeks in "Goathland" and the return of the wounded officers the Captain awarded me my watch keeping certificate and I received my next appointment to the big fleet destroyer "Meteor". She happened to be lying just astern of us alongside in Devonport dockyard, so it was just a walk to join her. Apart from a spell in hospital, I was to remain in "Meteor" until after the end of the war in August 1945.

I was nominally relieving the First Lieutenant but in practice the Second Lieutenant, who was also quite senior, relieved him and I took his place. The Captain, Lieutenant Commander Jewitt was the opposite of Pumphrey – a stickler for organisation and administration, soft with the ship's company but hard on his officers. He was also prejudiced against Reserve Officers of whom we had a RNR Lieutenant as Navigating Officer and three

RNVR Sub Lieutenants. Despite their greater age and experience, and the fact that I was still only a Sub Lieutenant RN I was nominated as Second Lieutenant and became Captain's Secretary, in charge of the ship's office, correspondence, pay and also Victualling Officer. In other words, I was to run the administration of the ship and had a Leading Writer in the office to assist and type, etc (although of necessity, I learned to type too and have never forgotten this). As a Seaman Officer, I was also Forecastle Officer, looked after the Forecastle Seaman's Division, was officer of the watch at Action Stations, stood my watch at sea (1 in 3) and Officers of the Day (OOD) in harbour. As Second Lieutenant I had a single cabin aft, next to the Captain's Day Cabin and opposite the First Lieutenant's so lived in far greater comfort than hitherto. When I first walked into the Wardroom I immediately recognized one of the RNVR Sub Lieutenants, Oliver Stirling-Lee, as an old Cheltonian. He was two years older than me and I hadn't known him at Cheltenham, but from then on we became good friends and remained so until his death in 2004.

"Meteor" was over 2000 tons and was armed with 6 unusual 4.7-inch guns, heavier than normal and fitted in 3 turrets or gun houses. We also carried torpedoes, a 4-inch AA gun and the usual outfit of depth charges. The Flotilla consisted of 7 ships ("Martin" having been lost during the North African landings) and was based with the Home Fleet at Scapa because large heavily armed destroyers were required to counter the heavy German "Narvik" class destroyers based in Norway with the battleship "Tirpitz", the battle cruiser "Scharnhorst" and other cruisers. Because of our heavy armament however, the 'M's were extremely wet in a seaway.

Soon after I joined, "Meteor" sailed for Scapa. That night I had the Middle Watch and as we were passing St Anne's Head at Milford Haven the Captain appeared on the bridge and demanded to know our position. Bearing in mind that no lighthouses functioned in wartime, I said "I think we are here", whereupon a heavy sea boot landed on my posterior and the Captain shouted that he didn't want to know what I thought; he wanted to know precisely where we were! Lesson learned and thereafter, I copied the other officers and took care to give him positive answers regardless of whether they were correct or not! One RNVR Sub Lieutenant, who was not very bright (but an Admiral's son), was frequently sent up the mast or the forecastle as a punishment for his inadequacies! Jewitt was a hard man and extremely unpopular in the Wardroom although considerate with the ships' company. As Forecastle Officer, I quickly discovered that the Captain was a very timid ship handler who rarely brought the ship in close enough when going alongside. As a result, I always had to have the Gunner's Mate on the Forecastle with the Coston Gun which fired a line over to the jetty or ship or wherever we were trying to get alongside. Throughout the destroyers at Scapa, the Captain was known as "*Coston Gun Jewitt*". However, not until some years later, did I realize how much he taught me about the tactical handling of a destroyer at sea and the administration and organisation of a destroyer and to some extent the Navy itself.

"Meteor" had been on one Russian convoy, PQ 18, before I joined but during the summer of 1943, there were no Russian convoys because the threat from the German Surface Forces, U-boats and air force in the perpetual Arctic daylight was far too serious to make it worthwhile. We spent some time in the Faroe Islands operating with RAF Coastal Command in an attempt to intercept and sink U-boats transiting through the Iceland/Faroes gap en route from Germany into the Atlantic. On detecting a U-boat, the aircraft would home our force of 3 or 4 destroyers onto its position. It nearly worked on one occasion but was later abandoned. In early October, our Polish manned sister ship "Orkan" (previously "Myrmidon") was sunk by the new German acoustic torpedo, known as the Gnat, whilst convoying in the Atlantic.

CHAPTER 5

THE RUSSIAN CONVOYS

IN NOVEMBER 1943, we were sent to the Wallsend Slipway at Newcastle-Upon-Tyne for a 6 week refit. Another new experience, and this time in a busy commercial yard where the Manager wore a bowler hat and was named Mr Rivet! We all had 10 days leave, and it was after returning that I went to a Red Cross Ball in Newcastle where I met my future wife, Alice. The rest of the refit went by as a dream, but it was soon back to Scapa. The Russian convoys were about to restart. As previously mentioned, "Meteor" had been involved in PQ18 before I joined – a famous convoy fought through to Murmansk with a very large escort after the disaster of PQ17 when it was dispersed. From now on, convoys left regularly every 2 weeks or so and were escorted alternately by the 3rd DF ('M' class) or the 17th DF ('O' class) destroyers of the Home Fleet augmented by other destroyers temporarily at Scapa for 'working up' and an escort force from the Western approaches at Liverpool. The convoys, usually consisting of 30-40 ships would come up to Iceland from Liverpool or Glasgow, or America/Canada with their escorts and then would be joined by the Home Fleet destroyers from Scapa before facing the German air/U-boat/surface ship threats from Norway. Other destroyers would escort the covering cruiser and battleship groups so that each convoy became a major operation involving many ships. It being winter there was virtually no daylight and my most abiding memory of those convoys was the frequent gales of unbelievable severity with seas which came at the ship from an angle of 40 degrees or so above the bridge (itself 40ft above sea level). In a head sea, seas would break over the forecastle then bounce up 'A' and 'B' turrets and finally, still solid green water, over the bridge by which time the Officer of the watch and the bridge crew would duck into whatever shelter they could find. In the worst weather, it even became impossible, when coming on or off watch to move aft to the Wardroom and cabins, so we lived in the CPO's mess until the weather abated. On one occasion, when I was going aft after a watch, I was caught by a sea coming in on the iron deck, lost my hold on the lifeline and was swept aft into one of the depth charge throwers on the Quarterdeck – I was very lucky not to go overboard.

Occasionally, we had to refuel at sea. This was done by what was called "*the astern method*", whereby the tanker would stream the fuel hose astern and we would close in, get the tail line by grapnel and haul the hose up on to the fo'c's'le. It would be connected to our forecastle fuel line. All this is not as easy as it sounds. In heavy weather, it was dangerous if a wave came over the forecastle, and also exceedingly difficult to catch the hose line with a grapnel. After it was caught, it required all my fo'c's'le seamen to haul the heavy hose up. Once connected, the Officer of the Watch then had to keep the ship exactly on station for an hour or more to avoid stretching or breaking the hose from the tanker. This method has long since been abandoned in favour of the "*the abeam method*" when the ship stations alongside the tanker, whose crane carries the hose over.

At this point, I might also mention the subject of clothing – extremely important for Seamen for both wet and rough weather and the extreme cold in northern waters. For most of the war, we wore oilskins and souwesters and/or duffle coats with hoods or sheepskin lined coats. They were uncomfortable to say the least and the sheepskins were extremely heavy and exhausting after a 4 hour watch standing on an open bridge. Then quite suddenly, in I think early 1944, we were supplied with new and novel 'anorak' kits. These consisted of a woollen undergarment with an anorak jacket with hood and trousers which came over the jacket and tied. The jacket had no buttons, was put on over the head and the whole ensemble was extremely light, waterproof, and above all, windproof. The forerunner of, I suppose, modern ski clothing and an absolute godsend. One also wore a pusser's life jacket (a cloth-covered rubber blow up tube) with a whistle and a red light so that you could be seen and heard if you should end up in the drink. Underneath all this, anything went and I personally wore a blue battledress and sweaters together with fur flying boots, which I had bought in London. The clothing stayed on at all times while we were at sea (including in one's bunk) and one of the first pleasures on reaching harbour, after as many as 10 days at sea, was to strip off and get into a hot

bath. The other secondary pleasures were the receipt of mail and drink –
lots of it as the strain of being at sea under constant threat of air and
submarine attack, etc, wore off. Incidentally, seaman officers never drank
at sea (although the Chief and Doctor were known to have a tipple and the
ship's company had their rum). Because of my ship duties, attending to the
correspondence, Ship's office, ship's company pay and victualling etc, I was
always extremely busy in harbour, but at Scapa was the destroyer depot
ship "Tyne", which held our pay accounts etc and where I could usually get
help and advice when needed. In those days too, after every 500 hours (later
750) at sea, our boilers had to be cleaned and this took about 4 days,
alternately alongside "Tyne" at Scapa, or joy of joys down south at Rosyth
or Glasgow where 48 hours leave was given. In the spring of 1944, when our
turn came, we were incredibly lucky and were sent instead to Newcastle-
Upon-Tyne, where I had a second spell meeting with my future wife Alice.

One of my biggest problems in "Meteor" was the victualling. In those
days, small ships ran on what was called 'canteen messing'. Everyone had a
daily victualling allowance and each mess appointed a caterer who
organized his menus and obtained his food from the Pusser and the NAAFI
Canteen. After preparation it was then taken to the galley for cooking. The
Pusser's victualling was run by the Stores Petty Officer who had to prepare
and present accounts at the end of each month. Our Stores PO was a stolid
West Countryman, honest but with limited abilities. There were always
errors and the Captain insisted on lengthy enquiries which took up much
precious time. Another problem was potatoes. Before every Russian convoy
we always took on and stored in the open upper deck storage five tons of
spuds. Alas, the freezing weather up north was too much for them and
invariably, after a few days, the frost got them and the whole lot would have
to be shoveled overboard. Another chore for me was the Captain's insistence
that I accompany the Coxwain (the senior rating in the ship) every day to
the Spirit Room to pump up the day's rum ration from the rum barrels
stored there. The compartment was very small, one had to crouch and the
stench of rum was blinding. I have never liked rum ever since. All this
perhaps makes the point that while fighting the war makes the headlines,
ships companies have to be fed, clothed, paid and organized so that they
have sufficient rest to sustain them over long periods.

To return to the convoys, our first that winter was JW55A consisting of
19 ships with a heavy close escort and support from a cruiser force and the

battleship "Duke of York". We joined on 15th December and reached the Kola inlet on the 21st. We left on the 23rd with the returning convoy RA55A and by 25th December became aware that the German battle cruiser "Scharnhorst" was at sea and threatening both our convoy and the next eastbound convoy JW55B. By the middle of Christmas morning, the two convoys had passed each other and the other was the threatened one. Our flotilla leader Captain D3 in "Milne" who was escort Commander, called for fuel returns and we guessed that some of our escorts, with the most fuel, would be switched to JW55B. A chance of action? Our Captain played it straight and we were not among the four destroyers ordered to join the other convoy. The destruction of the "Scharnhorst" and the part played by our sister ships "Musketeer" and "Matchless" is history. We faced a rising gale, one of the worst we experienced, which eventually completely scattered our convoy. Nearly home, we found ourselves completely on our own, but then ran into an old trawler from Aberdeen which had broken down. By this time the weather had moderated leaving only a heavy swell. The Captain sent me, accompanied by a Signalman, over to the trawler in the whaler to organise that end of the tow. The trawler had a full load of fish and lines of fish oil barrels round the upper deck. The lighting was by acetalyne and the Mate smoked a disgusting pipe. I had become a hardened sailor but succumbed to these obnoxious smells and the different motion of the trawler and was as sick as a dog! The tow however, was successful and 2 days later we reached Scapa where a tug relieved us of our burden. Many months later, "Meteor" was awarded salvage money. This is awarded on an established scale, the Captain getting the most down to the ordinary seamen the least. Because of my activity in the trawler, I got a double share – the princely sum of £3. 14 shillings!

On 28th January, we joined convoy JW56B of 17 ships. Three days later I happened to be Officer of the Watch (OOW) that evening when the senior Asdic operator suddenly reported "*Torpedo HE*" (hydrophone effect) 60 on our starboard bow as torpedoes were fired. Very fortunately, he was quick enough to enable me to turn the ship to comb the tracks. Because of our slow speed, this meant going 'full ahead' on the port engine and then, vitally, 'slow ahead' on both engines to avoid the torpedoes getting attracted to our propeller cavitations noise. The alarm bells had to be rung and the Captain also had to be called and he arrived on the bridge just in time to listen with bated breath to the HE noise on the loudspeaker of torpedoes passing down both sides of the ship and, thank God, no explosion. The Captain and the action Asdic team then took over, ran down the tracks, contact was made with the U-boat and depth charges fired. The destroyer "Whitehall" joined us and a long hunt and many attacks on the U-boat ensued until the hunt was finally abandoned towards midnight. The result was inconclusive and only after the war was it confirmed that we had sunk U.314. As it was, the Captain was convinced I had saved the ship from destruction (others having been lost to these dangerous homing torpedoes) and in May, after the Admiralty had agreed this deduction, the London Gazette announced the award of a DSM to A B Byrne (the Asdic Operator), and mentions in dispatches for E R A Bastin (for his prompt response to my manoeuvring orders), Oliver Stirling-Lee (the A/S Control Officer) and myself. Credit was also due to the Captain, Toby Jewitt, who had trained us all to a high standard and ensured we reacted automatically to an emergency. Later in the year, before he was relieved, he was awarded a DSC. The only other incident of note on that convoy was the sinking of "Hardy", a brand new flotilla header, but her ship's company was saved by brilliant ship handling by the Captain of "Venus", a sister ship, who put her alongside "Hardy" before she sank and took off her ship's company. The returning convoy RA56 got home safe and undetected.

On 22nd February 1944 we joined JW57, a very large convoy of over 40 ships with a large close escort including an aircraft carrier and cruiser carrying a Rear Admiral to command the operation. This was because the U-boat threat was increasing (there were 15 U-boats trying to get the previous convoy) and the escorts were increasingly under threat from the "gnat" homing torpedo. As it was, 3 days into the operation when I was again OOW that evening, our sister ship "Mahratta" was torpedoed. By this time incidentally we had all been fitted with TBS, a radio telephone, so we were able to hear what was going on. The Captain of "Mahratta" was reporting his situation. A nearby destroyer, "Impulsive" was offering to go alongside to take off her ship's company, but the Admiral was refusing to allow it. The night was very dark but the weather was calm and there was a bit of a swell running so the Admiral evidently thought it was too risky. A short time later, "Mahratta" was hit by a second torpedo, rolled over and sank. "Impulsive" and other escorts moved in to pick up survivors, but out of over 200, there were only 17 rescued. A vivid lesson to everyone, that if you are torpedoed and end up in the sea, the cold will kill you before you could be rescued. The Admiral's decision caused angry discussions in Wardrooms for weeks after this sad affair. We escorted the returning convoy RA57 losing only one ship and reaching Scapa on about 8th March. The next convoy JW58 included the American Cruiser "Milwaukee" which was to be handed over to the Russians. In April, a large force of escorts including "Meteor" sailed for the Kola Inlet in order to bring back over 40 empty ships, the crew of the "Milwaukee" and Russian crews for more ships to be taken over by them. On the return trip we had a US Navy Lieutenant Commander who had been the "Milwaukee" Gunnery Officer, as our guest and I remember being struck by the similarity of language, knowledge and attitude between us as professional Naval Officers. No further convoys sailed until August as most of the Home Fleet had gone south to cover the Normandy landings. We remained at Scapa and on 29th June, "Matchless", "Meteor", and "Musketeer" sailed on a fast run to Russia with supplies and mail etc., for personnel based up there. We were back in Scapa by 8th July and I remember how glorious the weather was on that summer trip with hours of daylight.

We did two more return convoys to Russia. The first JW59, after the Normandy landings, left on 17th August with 34 ships and the battleship "Archangel" (formerly HMS "Royal Sovereign"). The frigate "Kite" was sunk by a U-boat with heavy loss of life, but otherwise the escorts with the supporting carrier aircraft, were well on top of the U-boats and destroyed two. On this convoy, I remember as we approached the Kola Inlet one dark evening, we were threatened by some 20 U-boats round the convoy. The escort Commander, Captain Campbell in "Milne" ordered all escorts (about 18) to fire starshell outwards. The horizon all around the convoy became daylight, forcing the U-boats to dive and falling astern of the convoy. We returned in early September and on the 17th September we joined our last convoy JW60, escorting over 30 ships with returning RA60 back to Scapa in early October without incident.

Up to this time during the war, the Russian authorities at Murmansk had been distinctly unfriendly because of the lack of a second front and while waiting for the return convoys all the escorts were anchored after refueling, in Vaenga Bay, which was even more bleak than Scapa and without any facilities. On arrival with JW59 however, the atmosphere had changed completely (post Normandy) and 9 destroyers were invited to berth alongside 3 abreast in their naval base at Polyarnoe. The officers trooped up the hill for vodka and caviar in the Russian HQ with a return match in our ships the next day. As we were there for 3 days, a pulling regatta was organized, whalers were lowered and crews were organised and started training. The ships' doctors organised a tote, everyone relaxed and a typical spontaneous naval occasion was enjoyed by all. Back to the war the next day.

By September, the battleship "Tirpitz" was finally put out of action and the Luftwaffe moved south to defend Germany. So the surface and air threat to the convoys ceased and only the U-boat threat remained. More and more escorts and carriers were being built and becoming available. So there was no need for our flotilla, the largest destroyers in the Navy, with our large guns, to remain. We had taken part in 8 return convoys. I have not mentioned that between convoys, we were often at sea escorting the battleships and aircraft carriers of the Home Fleet in strikes against the "Tirpitz" or sweeps down the Norwegian coast. By the middle of 1944, Fleet Air Arm aircraft were unopposed and destroyed every ship they saw.

CHAPTER 6

MEDITERRANEAN BLISS

WE WERE DELIGHTED therefore when, sometime in September 1944, we were suddenly ordered south for leave and preparations for service in the Mediterranean. While at Devonport, our Captain, Lt Cdr Toby Jewitt, was relieved by Lt Cdr R D Pankhurst. The contrast was striking! Pankhurst, who spoke almost incoherently out of the corner of his mouth, took little interest in the ship or the ship's company, although he later showed he could handle the ship pretty well. Years later I acquired a book entitled "The Figurehead" written by Vice Admiral Sir Roderick MacDonald. In it he described his experiences as a Sub Lieutenant and Navigator of a destroyer earlier in the war, commanded by an unnamed officer, who I later heard was Pankhurst. His lack of interest in this ship almost led to his court martial. Personally I never got on with Pankhurst. However, after our leave, we were soon on our way to the Mediterranean and after brief stops at Gibraltar and Malta, arrived in Alexandria in Egypt about mid November.

This was my first time in the Eastern Mediterranean and after the bitter cold and appalling weather of the Arctic, it was sheer bliss. Very soon, we were sent up from Alexandria (Alex) to the Greek Dodecanese Islands where, by this time, the German Air Force and U-boats had withdrawn leaving only garrisons in the Islands. Our task was to harass these garrisons and with another destroyer "Kelvin" in company and with an SBS Captain embarked, we set about the Germans on the small island of Piskopi, just west of Rhodes. I recall the ship lying about a mile off the little town on the island while the SBS Captain, sitting in the Director with Ray Williams, our Australian GCO, trained our guns on to individual houses which were the Gestapo HQ or army HQ etc., and demolishing them with 2 gun salvoes at point blank range! Later we bombarded the German garrison, forced them to retire over the hill to the other side of the island, and then raced round to give them another pasting. After some days of this, we tried to get the garrison to surrender. The SBS Captain went ashore in our motor boat with a white flag and we covered him as he climbed towards the German forces. But they opened fire on him and he beat a hasty retreat, covered by salvoes from our guns. I remember also, and have a photograph, of officers rowing to a beach for a swim and of visiting the island of Symi (now a well known tourist resort) where it was only safe to enter if locals had hung a red carpet over the balcony of the Governor's Palace to indicate no Germans present. The weather was perfect, the location idyllic and we must have spent several weeks in the area. On our final night before returning to Alex, several destroyers joined the cruiser "Aurora" and, in pouring rain, carried out a blind radar controlled bombardment of Rhodes harbour, lasting about 20 minutes. In that time, about 3,000 shells would have been fired but we later heard that they missed the harbour and hit the town – such is war and the limitations of early Radar.

We had not been back in Alex long, when after the German withdrawal from Greece we heard that Civil War had broken out. British troops were sent from Italy and we and several sister ships were sent up from Alex. After arriving at Piraeus, the port of Athens, we watched RAF aircraft rocketing and bombing the communist EOKA forces. One of the pilots, I subsequently discovered, was Bill Youdale, whose farm at Etchingham I lived on in the 1970's. After a short stay we left to go to Kalamata in the Peleponnese while "Musketeer" went to Volos in the East. At Kalamata the Captain, who had witnessed the Irish troubles between the wars, tried the traditional naval approach to keeping the peace by inviting the leaders of both sides ELAS and EOKA, to gin and lunch with him in his cabin. At the end of which, both agreed to behave. And they did until a week or so later, strong communist EOKA forces were reported approaching from the north and we were ordered to evacuate the small British army force ashore and withdraw. One day, during our stay at Kalamata, there arrived on board 3 or 4 British Army Officers who belonged to the Liaison team with the Greek Guerilla forces fighting the Germans. Basically, they came for much needed baths and, of course, also enjoyed drinks and lunch in the Wardroom, but the interesting thing about their visit was that their kit was full of Socialist literature and the talk was all about the future Labour Government after the war! Our First Lieutenant was revealed to be a Labour enthusiast while the rest of us had hardly given our future Government a thought!

On our return to Alex in December 1944, I was diagnosed with a bad hernia and had to leave "Meteor" and go to a temporary naval hospital at the old Casino at San Stefano. There I had my operation, the then obligatory 3 weeks in bed and several more weeks in a convalescent guesthouse in Alex. I was then appointed to the small boat maintenance depot in Alex harbour for the also obligatory 3 months shore service. I forget what my duties were in this extraordinary establishment, but it was commanded by a South African Lt Cdr and manned by a mixture of Palestinian and Jewish mechanics, some of whom were refugees from German industry and very highly skilled. The job was to maintain the large number of small craft that serviced all the functions of a major naval base such as Alex. In due course, I was passed fit to return to "Meteor" who by this time was supporting the army in northern Italy. I took passage in a captured Italian cruiser and remember her superb build and interior fittings – all gleaming aluminium, etc. Memorably, we arrived in Malta on 8th May (VE Day) where I witnessed across Grand Harbour, drunken fleet air arm crews pushing their aircraft over the side into the harbour! I then took passage to Naples and somewhere, I remember not where, rejoined "Meteor". Sadly, I missed "Meteor's" finest hour a month or so earlier, when, with the destroyer "Lookout" she had met three German manned Italian destroyers off Corsica. In a sharp high speed night action on opposite courses, "Meteor" had sunk one by torpedoes and gunfire. The Captain and Ray Williams, our Australian GCO since the ship was first commissioned, got very well earned DSCs. There had been changes in the Wardroom and I was hardly welcomed back by our strange Captain. I was given no job to do. However, soon after I returned, our new Captain (D), Captain Richmond, had the bright idea of taking the surviving ships of the flotilla, "Milne", "Musketeer", "Marne", "Matchless", and "Meteor" to Elba, where there is good anchorage, for a period of "general drill". This is a peacetime activity designed to sharpen ships up and get them on their toes. By the end of the war, ships were manned by about 80% 'hostilities only' ship's companies and while something had to be done to keep men occupied until their turn for demobilisation came, their only interest was just that. So the choice of general drill was insensitive to say the least, and I remember a very difficult week with our new First Lieutenant Richard Wilson requiring all the support he could get from the officers. As it was, "Marne" had a mutiny which ruined the careers of her Captain (an old Cheltonian) and First Lieutenant. The only pleasant memories I have of Elba are the ambience and beauty of the bay and a lunch given by a charming Italian Countess for some of us in her exquisite villa on the hill overlooking the bay. Later, I recall going ashore at Santa Margarita, on the Italian Riviera, and finding bodies everywhere, victims of the revenge of the Resistance against the Italian fascists etc.

CHAPTER 7

BACK TO THE UK

T HAT FOR ME, was the end of the war. My hernia had unbelievably recurred after 3 months and our young RNVR Ships' Doctor, recognizing its seriousness, arranged for me to be invalided home. I left "Meteor" at Marseilles and I was one of the first servicemen to return by rail, from Marseilles to Dieppe, with a change in Paris, after the bridges and track etc., had been repaired. Then ferry to Newhaven and finally to Cooden near Bexhill, where my parents had recently retired, just five years after I joined the Royal Navy and just before VJ Day in August 1945.

Like all my contemporaries and despite our much shortened training, I was now a fully qualified Lieutenant RN with two years seniority. I had perforce learned the basics of my profession very fast. I had survived four areas of pretty fierce combat; the Java Sea battle, the North African invasion, E-boat fighting in the channel and the Russian convoys. Three of my RN term mates had been killed and three RCN Midshipmen as well.

My father, a retired GP, insisted that my hernia should be dealt with privately and he and the local GP arranged for a Consultant Surgeon to come down to Bexhill Hospital. After the operation, he told my father that he had never seen such a mess and could not be sure he had put it 100% right. After convalescence, I was appointed a divisional officer at HMS "St George" in the Isle of Man on 13th November 1945. This was the boys' training establishment which had been evacuated from HMS "Ganges" near Ipswich. "St George" was a hutted holiday camp and I took over 250 boys in Hawke Division from Teddy Gueritz, another old Cheltonian. However, during the following Christmas leave, the whole establishment was moved back to HMS "Ganges". Unfortunately, the last conscripts who had been trained there, broke the place up before leaving and we were faced with formidable problems. Apart from the damage, there were serious organisation problems starting from scratch. The Commander wisely decided to use the pre-war order book and organisation and we went from there. There were 8 divisions totaling some 2,000 boys. The eight Divisional Officers were all 'crocks' – shore service only while recovering from war wounds, operations or illnesses. Our deputies were all temporary Warrant Officers while each division was divided into 4 double classes each with two CPO or PO instructors. The boys were an extraordinary mixture ranging from Glasgow razor gangs to Public School boys. The routine was, of course vigorous and complex, ranging through daily divisions, instruction classes, PT and swimming instruction and games.

Alas, sometime that spring, the Admiralty Medical Board refused to pass me as fit and furthermore, threatened that unless my hernia was rectified, I would be invalided. A supreme irony since the Navy had been responsible for the failure of the first operation. I later discovered that the 'Surgical Specialist' at the Royal Naval Hospital (RNH) in Alex did not actually have any surgical specialisation, only the standard Doctor's qualifications. The Admiralty Medical board would not, of course, admit any liability. It was a wartime situation and would not be treated that way nowadays. So back to Bexhill where in May 1946 the same surgeon tried again. In August, after convalescence, I joined HMS "Dolphin" the submarine base at Gosport for my shore service. Here I was Divisional Officer for a large number of submariners, many of whom were awaiting demobilization after the war. I was also the Commander's Assistant and this proved interesting. One morning I was with the Commander in his office when the Paymaster Commander came in (Supply Officer in modern parlance). He had been checking victualling accounts and regretted to report that 40 gallons of rum was missing! The Commander scoffed and said "try the other one", but it became evident that this really was the case! The Commander ordered me to start investigating but after some days I had to confess that I was getting nowhere. So the Commander tried and also failed. A NAAFI Investigator was called in, an ex-detective. No one enquired about his methods but at length he got a confession out of someone. It transpired that for years, the Royal Marine security guards, who had access to the keys, had been filching rum from the store at night, and it was then traded throughout HMS "Dolphin" and even ashore. It led to some half dozen courts martial and sadly, court convictions at the

Gosport Magistrates Court against several pensioners who worked in "Dolphin". It also nearly queered the career of our popular Captain as it was revealed that he was having a fruit spraying machine made in the engineering workshop for the farm to which he was soon retiring.

While all this was going on, my romance with Alice in Newcastle was developing and we finally got married at St George's Church in Jesmond Newcastle-upon-Tyne on 30th December 1946, followed by a honeymoon in a hotel in a snowy Lake district at Keswick, which had its own farm and fabulous food – a rarity in those days of rationing. Oliver Stirling-Lee from "Meteor" days was my best man and many years later, after his death, his widow told me that if I hadn't married Alice, he would have wished to! On returning to Gosport I managed to find a little semi basement flat in Southsea and Alice joined me for a most idyllic last few months of my time at "Dolphin". On 16th April 1947 I was passed fit for general service and so this worrying time of nearly two years was over and I could continue my career in the RN.

CHAPTER 8
THE MEDITERRANEAN AGAIN

I WENT TO the Admiralty to see my Appointer. "I am going to send you to "Liverpool" in the Med," he said.

"Oh" said I, "could I not go to something smaller?"

"Young man," said this Senior Commander, "you are going to the Fleet Flagship so consider yourself lucky." He was quite right and I was chastened! We packed up the flat, Alice returned to Newcastle, and I caught a troopship at Liverpool on 4th July 1947. I arrived in Malta and joined "Liverpool", a 10,000 ton cruiser with nine 6-inch guns and by far the largest ship I had ever served in. I became the Top Divisional Officer and Boat Officer, i.e. responsible for the middle section of the upper deck. There was watch keeping both at sea and on the quarter deck in harbour. I also became the Plot Officer working with the Navigating Officer on planning and executing all the many exercises carried out at sea, under the direction of the Commander-in-Chief (C-in-C).

On 11th July 1947, we sailed for Phaleron Bay in Greece near Athens with C-in-C on board – Admiral Sir Algernon Willis. There, I attended a ball at the British Embassy, cocktails and tennis parties and we entertained the King and Queen of Greece on board. Then on to Sevastopol for a visit with the Russians, exchanging a cocktail party on board for a traditional Russian song and dance concert in a hall ashore which was just about the only building standing in Sevastopol after the terrible fighting during the war. No Russians spoke English, nor we Russian but the British Embassy in Moscow sent down some Russian speakers to interpret. Back to peacetime naval activities, what a change to the war and of course a new experience for me. From Sevastopol, we went to Nauplia in Greece where virtually the whole Mediterranean fleet had gathered for the Fleet Regatta. Then on to

Cyprus for bombardment practice at Cape Arnauti and visits to Larnaca and Famagusta. Back to Malta on 22nd August after intensive exercises en route. We then had a spell in dry dock before sailing to Gibraltar on 19th September. Then up to Toulon for a visit where I recall visiting Bandol for some swimming and a night club in Toulon that evening. By this time, we had been informed that "Liverpool" was to return to Chatham and pay off for a refit and, soon after, we made our way home, reaching Chatham at the end of October 1947. Most of the Executive Officers then moved, more or less together, to Devonport to commission "Newcastle", a sister ship. However, "Newcastle" had been in dockyard hands for a long time, was filthy and still had wartime paint everywhere, including the decks. So we had a huge task to get the ship fit for service in the Mediterranean. I was given the Quarterdeck Division and continued as Watchkeeper at sea and in harbour. Most of the Wardroom had come from "Liverpool" and the whole commission turned out to be one of the happiest I ever experienced. I rented a small flat from a French lady in Plymouth and Alice joined me for a brief stay until we sailed for Malta. By that time, Alice's passage to Malta had also been fixed so we had much to look forward to. On passage to Malta, the Commander gave instructions that the after screens (or superstructures) were to be painted with light grey enamel, a much superior finish. So the old paint was chipped off, a long and laborious job, and red lead primer applied. Then, days went by and the red lead would not set! Time was short and it was then discovered that the painter had issued non-setting red lead which is normally used in the bilges! Panic, as it all had to be cleaned off and proper red lead applied. Time ran out and the flagship sailed into Grand Harbour, Malta, covered in red lead! In the ensuing weeks we got it right, the decks clear of paint and scrubbed daily and the brass work gleaming.

We were fit to take the C-in-C on an official visit to Jeddah, the summer capital of Saudi Arabia in the Red Sea. Sometime later the C-in-C relinquished "Newcastle" which became the flagship of the 1st Cruiser Squadron, commanded by Rear Admiral Symonds-Taylor. A very 'hands-on' sailor and I recall that sometime in 1948, the entire flag signalling system in the Royal Navy was changed to a new system based on that in the US Navy. The Executive Officers were required to stand with the Admiral on the quarterdeck and read hoists of the new flags put up by the Chief Yeoman on the flag deck. A thorough knowledge was essential at sea as radio communications were still not fully developed and flags were still used for manoeuvring, etc.

In May 1948, Alice arrived in Malta in the troopship "Empress of Scotland". Also on board were the Captains' wife and his two charming teenage daughters. Initially, Alice stayed in the Osborne hotel in South Street, Valetta, next to Admiralty House, the home of C-in-C. Malta was, of course, still in ruins after the war and accommodation was exceedingly difficult to find. We eventually managed to rent half of the Villa Ta Xbiex, on a little peninsular between Msida and Lazeretto Creeks. A nice area and we had a lovely first floor bedroom and bathroom, but our living room was the wash house on the roof. A rough structure with a corrugated iron roof! When it rained on that roof, you could not hear anything! Alice managed to get some old furniture from the Osborne hotel basement and it was then that I first learned of her amazing ability to make a home out of next to nothing! She was a true naval wife.

From then on life developed a pattern; we would be away for up to 6 weeks at a time and then back to our buoys in Grand Harbour. There were other wives in Malta and life was hectic and fun with beach, swimming and cocktail parties, etc. Our visits around the Mediterranean were a mixture of crises e.g., in Trieste and the Haifa Patrol dealing with illegal Jewish immigrants, or official visits to Beirut or Greece or Palermo in Sicily or Algiers or, in August, to Golfe Juan in the South of France to name a few. I recall our Captain of Royal Marines going ashore in Beirut dressed in arab clothes and later being chased back to the ship by a mob. What he had done I never discovered. I have a photo of him driving his motorbike around my precious quarterdeck. At Golfe Juan on some evenings a party of officers would take the motor boat round to Cannes harbour where we would debark into the nearby casino, each armed with the equivalent of about 50p. We played roulette and when you lost, you stopped. If you won you stood the drinks. Late in 1948, Rear Admiral Symonds-Taylor was relieved by Rear Admiral Mountbatten. He had returned from his time in India as Viceroy and Governor General and immediately impressed with his arrogance, charm and personality. He had the dockyard put the crests of all the 14th Army units he had had under his command in Burma during the war around his cabin. He came with an extra secretary to cope with his continuing correspondence with the Prime Minister Clement Attlee, as a junior Rear Admiral! He went round the Fleet lecturing on the Transfer of

Power in India and over time, he entertained every officer in the squadron to lunch. Within a comparatively short time, he succeeded in gathering all four cruisers in the squadron together in Malta for the first time and then carried out spectacular high speed gridiron manoeuvres outside Malta – ever the showman. In the spring of 1949 he commanded the Mediterranean fleet in the manoeuvres with the Home Fleet off Gibraltar after a very rough passage from Malta during which his car on the boat deck was severely damaged. The Countess of Mountbatten set up house at their old home, the Villa Guadamangia, with a huge staff including 2 Indian Bearers. She entertained all the officer's wives and my nervous Alice was put completely at ease by her charm and graciousness. Just before Christmas 1948 the Admiral informed Stuart Paton, our Captain, that the Countess would join him in the traditional mess deck rounds on Christmas morning. "Very well" said Stuart Paton, "then my officers shall be accompanied by their wives". Thus what I believe was a unique event took place, since wives had never before been on the mess decks. The ship's company reacted magnificently. "Newcastle" was a happy ship and we spent the entire forenoon amongst our sailors on the mess decks. Indeed, it was 3pm before we eventually sat down for our own Christmas lunch in the Wardroom.

Lest it be thought that life in "Newcastle" was all fun and games, the first Commander (or Executive Officer) was a ruthless and ambitious man who expected and got the highest standards from everyone. My quarterdeck particularly had to be immaculate. At 6.30 every morning the deck was scrubbed, occasionally with holystone, the brightwork cleaned and the paintwork washed. My first Divisional Petty Officer was not very good and the Commander then gave me an experienced Chief Petty Officer who was quite superb. It took some 20 men to haul the huge quarterdeck awning over the Stay and set it up and this had to be done at precisely the same moment as wires went ashore or we anchored. The quarterdeck then had to be spick and span within minutes, ready to receive distinguished visitors of which there were many. At almost every port visited, we would hold a reception or cocktail party for which a ceremonial awning was spread under the main awning and side curtains hung. The morale of my quarterdeck men became very high and amongst their achievements was the winning of the ship's regatta. As a further example of the standard required I once went ashore in Grand Harbour Malta to be met by Alice and we strolled along the road towards the Custom House and the Baraka Lift, with my arm around her waist. The next morning, the Commander summoned me and gave me a tremendous rocket for my unbecoming behaviour ashore! Thus were the standards of conduct in the Royal Navy restored to peacetime levels after having slipped considerably during the war. I was very aware of this need and felt no resentment – polish was needed.

Early in 1949 Alice became pregnant and later in the year this presented a problem. I was due to be relieved in July, but Alice was not allowed to travel by troop ship when over 5 months pregnant. My Captain, Stuart Paton, knew of the situation and sent for me not long before he himself was relieved. "Would I like to stay in the Mediterranean?" he asked, and on my affirmative, said he would see what he could arrange. Not long after, I was appointed First Lieutenant of the frigate "Peacock" round in Sliema Creek, exactly what I would have wished in my desire to get back to small ships.

I left "Newcastle" on 13th July 1949 after a most happy and rewarding two years in cruisers, having learned a great deal about the peacetime Navy and served with a magnificent bunch of officers and men. After two weeks station leave, I joined "Peacock" where it rapidly became apparent that her Captain had requested that his First Lieutenant be relieved! He and two other lieutenants were all emergency service officers retained after the war. They lacked the social graces among other things and various incidents had led to all Wren officers and ratings being forbidden to accept invitations to "Peacock". The party that greeted my arrival was drunken, and it was clearly going to be a challenge. In those 'Black Swan' class frigates the Wardroom was aft but the Captain lived forward under the Bridge, so he had little idea what his officers were up to. The Captain, Nigel Willmott was a Senior Commander, who had been heavily decorated during the war for organising the survey of enemy beaches in Sicily, Italy and Normandy prior to the invasions. He had a farm near Ditchling in East Sussex, which his wife was running. "Peacock" spent a lot of time as Guardship in Aqaba in the Red Sea. We were there to support the British Army battalion ashore and to keep the peace in an area where the borders of Saudi Arabia, Jordan, Israel and Egypt all reach the sea at the head of the Gulf of Aqaba and within a few miles of each other. With our six 4-inch guns we were capable of giving substantial bombardment support but fortunately it was never necessary. During my time in "Peacock" we did three or four spells there and the passage through the Suez Canal became very familiar. On our last visit we found the Sussex Regiment on duty and when they heard that both the Captain and I came from the county, we were invited to a Regimental dinner. This was held under canvas, in the desert, accompanied by the regimental band and with all the regimental silver on the table! An amazing performance! Returning from one of our Aqaba visits, we picked up a journalist in Port Said for passage to Malta. He stayed in the Captain's cabin. One afternoon, the Captain's Maltese Steward appeared at my cabin door and said that the Captain and his guest were going to jump overboard! I walked up to the bridge and as I got there, there was a loud shout below and the pair of them duly did jump overboard! The lifebuoy alarm was pressed and the lifebuoy thrown overboard. The lifeboat crew was called away, the ship turned and in due course, Captain and guest were back on board. Our two emergency List Lieutenants had by this time, been relieved by two young Acting Sub Lieutenants and one of these inexperienced youngsters was Officer of the Watch. I never did discover whether the Captain's Steward took it upon himself to warn me or whether the Captain himself had sent him. Typical of him though to exercise the ship in this way. When I told some of my chums back in Malta, I was jocularly told that I should have left them (the Captain was not very popular)!

Life was busy in "Peacock" as I had much reorganising to do but life went pretty smoothly. One day, I was mustering the victualling stores and discovered that the front row of Pusser's tobacco tins on a shelf disguised the fact that there were no more tins behind as there should have been. Other items were also missing. Further investigation revealed that the stores PO had an arrangement at Port Said with the Egyptian supplier of fresh food, 'Jim Irish', whereby only one ton of potatoes was received on board when two tons had been ordered, the profit being split between them. Inevitably the stores Petty Officer was court martialled in Malta, given a prison sentence and dismissed from the service.

In October 1949 while we were returning to Malta from, I think, Venice, Alice gave birth to our first born, Simon, at the Blue Sisters Nursing Home in Malta. The naval family doctor was there, but both he and the Sisters were strict Roman Catholics and did not believe in any pain relievers, so poor Alice had a tough time. I did not reach Malta until two days later, but better late than never!

In May 1950, the Captain was relieved by a very charming 4-stripe Captain, with whom I got on extremely well. It was he, as a Commander, who had saved the "Hardy's" ships company on that Russian convoy. His wife was also equally charming with Alice. By this time incidentally, Prince Philip, who had been First Lieutenant of "Chequers" the leader of the Destroyer flotilla in Malta became Captain of our chummy ship "Magpie". I met Prince Philip for the first time at a First Lieutenant's meeting in "Chequers" to discuss the disposal of pig swill by ships in Sliema Creek! Princess Elizabeth was also in Malta but the social whirl around the Royals and the Mountbattens largely passed us by in Sliema Creek. We did go to the occasional destroyer or frigate party, but we were away from Malta an awful lot. Alice had her hands full with Simon and we also had a dog, a stray that Alice had taken in, and two cats! One of these trips away was to the Fleet Regatta in Greece. We had prepared hard for this and were extremely successful in winning the small ships part of it, a great boost to the morale of the ship. One day with the ship in Sliema Creek, Malta, I was with Captain Richardson in his cabin when there was a tremendous thump, the whole ship shook and the lights went out. I rushed down to discover that our auxiliary diesel generator, which is used when the boilers are shut down in the harbour, had suffered a con rod failure. Unusually, the con rod had fractured at the top which left the rod, on the next revolution, to drive through the casing and break the generator into two parts, with one part lifted off its base. Since the generator was about six feet high, this was a massive failure and necessitated a move to Malta dockyard to have a replacement fitted.

Sometime that summer, we were informed that we would have a refit at Gibraltar, proceeding direct from our next visit to Aqaba. At the same time I was informed that I would be relieved in Gibraltar. This presented a domestic problem yet again, but Alice somehow managed to pack all our belongings and arrange a troopship passage to Gibraltar. We were reunited in Gibraltar in September 1950. We had also purchased a small car in Malta which was shipped home in an aircraft carrier.

We stayed at the 'Bristol' Hotel and after all the preparations for the refit and discussions of our defect lists and alterations and additions list, the refit got underway. Following the arrival of my relief, we expected to be shipped home, but unfortunately the Korean War had started and every available troopship was employed ferrying troops to the Far East. We were stuck in the hotel for about six weeks, slowly going broke as the cost far exceeded my pay and allowances. Eventually, we got a passage in an old

RFA store ship and crawled home at about 10 knots. After 3½ years away in the Mediterranean, we eventually berthed at, of all places, the coal wharf in Chatham Dockyard, and flat broke! Two taxis took us and our baggage to my parent's home in Bexhill where we spent our Foreign Service leave. During that leave I was appalled to receive an appointment to the aircraft carrier "Vengeance", which was not even flying aircraft and where I supposed I would be Mate of the upper deck and perhaps doing more watchkeeping. I knew I would not be happy in this appointment and asked if it could be changed. Just at this time and fortunate for me but most unfortunate for those concerned, a dreadful accident occurred at Setubal in Portugal, which the 5th destroyer squadron was visiting. One evening, four officers set off from the ships to attend a reception. The car was driven over the edge and into the dock and they all drowned. One of them was the First Lieutenant of "St Kitts" and so it came about that my appointment was changed and I joined this 'Battle' class destroyer in Chatham dockyard on 4th January 1951 as First Lieutenant. By that time, and after a long and difficult search in an area we did not know, Alice and I found a small house in the village of Rainham near Gillingham Kent, where we happily settled for the next 2½ years.

CHAPTER 9

THE HOME FLEET

THIS APPOINTMENT SUITED me perfectly and of the six destroyers in the squadron I discovered that while I was still a Lieutenant and 28 years old, the other five First Lieutenants were all Lieutenant Commanders. My Captain, G A G Ormsby, was a Senior Commander heavily decorated for U-boat sinkings during the war, but very quiet and reticent. In the Home Fleet, we were invariably away from Chatham except for the three leave periods each year, so I probably saw less of the family than in the Mediterranean. The spring cruise each year was traditionally to Gibraltar for the combined Fleet exercises with the Mediterranean Fleet. The summer of 1951 was the Festival of Britain and the Home Fleet took part, visiting ports all round the UK. "St Kitts" visited Portrush in Northern Ireland where the British Open Golf was taking place; Filey in Yorkshire; Folkestone, where my family came to see us, and finally Southampton, where we joined our Squadron leader "Solebay". At Filey, the Commanding Officer and officers were invited to dinner at the local Butlins holiday camp. The Captain rightly decided that this was not for him and delegated me to go with three or four other officers. We were in mess undress and because there was no jetty or pier to land at, had to remove our socks and shoes and paddle ashore. We then walked up the beach to the camp where, after wandering around for a while, we found someone and told them who we were. Bear in mind that we were all dressed for dinner in bum freezer jackets and bow ties. "Oh well, you had better come and have a meal". So we sat in solitary splendour, had our Butlins meal and we then returned to the beach and the ship's motor boat.

On 31st July 1951, we had a new Captain, Eroll Sinclair, tall, bearded and self-opinionated. He was an experienced small ship hand, but had been ashore since the war and was thus a little out of date, so initially we clashed. But we settled down and "St Kitts" went well for the next 18 months.

On 5th September 1951 we left Chatham for the Home Fleet Autumn Cruise and fortunately stopped at Spithead to collect some urgently needed spares. I was able to nip ashore and telephone home where I learned that Alice had given birth to our second son Philip, that day in a Gillingham nursing home. Soon after, we were ordered to join the Aircraft Carrier "Ocean" as 'Plane Guard'. In those days before the advent of the angled flight deck and mirror landing lights, the heavy aircraft then flying were often too strong for the barriers and if something went wrong with their deck landings, quite frequently they ended up in the drink. The attendant destroyer then had to act very quickly to rescue the aircrew. "Ocean" was working up her Air Group while en route to the Korean war and we stayed with her all the way through the Mediterranean, the Suez Canal and the Red Sea ending up in Aden where another escort took over 'Plane Guard'. Aden must have been the furthest that any Home Fleet ship had ever reached and it was nearly Christmas before we eventually returned to Chatham for the leave period.

Early in 1952, we were informed that "St Kitts" had been selected to accompany the battleship "Vanguard" on the King's second convalescent trip to South Africa later that year. I arranged with Chatham Dockyard to have various wooden fittings, such as gratings fitted to smarten the upper deck and a new carpet for the Wardroom etc. Very sadly, while exercising off Gibraltar during the Spring Cruise, we heard that the King had died. We never got our fittings or carpets but I have a photo to celebrate the cruise that never happened.

During my two years in "St Kitts" we experimented with an interesting innovation in the tactical handling of the ship during exercises at sea. Nowadays, with fully developed and equipped operations rooms, Captains operate from that room and not from the bridge which is now covered and solely for conning and manoeuvring the ship. Both my Captains decided to experiment with this as yet untried method, bearing in mind that radar and plotting were not as advanced as now. So the Captain was below controlling the ship while I was stationed on the open bridge as a safety number. This was all very well, but at night I had to depend on binoculars to ensure that we avoided colliding with anyone while charging around the ocean at 30 knots. At times this got quite hairy, but, as far as I can remember, only once did I have to intervene with an emergency course alteration.

"St Kitts" had two characters. One was the oldest Able Seaman in the Royal Navy, George Parker. I forget why he had been allowed to extend his service but he had a typical 'Players (cigarettes) Please' beard and was a credit to the service. Before going on leave he used to arrange for someone to send a recall telegram, so that he was rarely at home for more than 48 hours. He was the Chief Boatswains mate's locker man and a dreadful squirrel! During a short refit in Chatham dockyard a welder caused a fire – in George's store. This gave the Buffer and me the chance to have a serious huck out. We could never have done it without such an excuse! George was eventually pensioned after 34 years of service.

The other character was a little miniature brass cannon we had in the Wardroom. It had been made on the island of St Kitts from the brass of a real cannon raised from the sea bed at the site of the battle of St Kitts in 1782. It was an exact replica and fired 'Pussers Peas' (hard marrowfat peas) with devastating effects (grape shot). This little gun was no more than 6-inches long and we evolved a form of gun drill for use on guest night dinners or our battle night (25th January) which was always a big Wardroom occasion.

During my nearly 2 years in "St Kitts" I took the various parts of the Destroyer Command exam. These consisted of supply, administration, gunnery, damage control, communications, torpedo and anti-submarine and navigation in two parts. The navigation was the toughest, but I finally made it in November 1952 just before I was relieved. It was difficult to find time during one's normal duties to prepare for all these subjects, some written and some oral, but my six years in destroyers and frigates provided a sound base and I stretched it out, taking two subjects at a time, so I was now qualified to command a ship.

I left "St Kitts" in December 1952 but after Christmas was admitted to RNH Chatham for yet another hernia operation (on the opposite side to the earlier one). The Surgical Specialist at RNH Chatham happened to be the Surgeon who accompanied the King on his trips abroad in the Royal Yacht "Britannia" and with a first class reputation, so I felt happy to return to the Navy for this one. In the event, this faith was fully justified and I never had any further trouble after this operation.

On 16th March 1953 I was appointed temporarily to the Coronation Naval Review Staff at Portsmouth to help plan the Review, due later that summer. The Commodore in Command was none other than my first 'Snottie's Nurse' in HMS "Danae" 12 years previously, Joe Blackham, and my job was to allocate landing places and tenders for the libertymen of the dozens of ships attending the Review. A month later I was in the Admiralty being briefed by the Naval Intelligence Division as I had been appointed to the Staff of the C-in-C Far East on his Intelligence Staff. Soon after, we packed our belongings at Rainham to go to Singapore, let the house to a friend and moved temporarily to a flat in Bexhill before leaving for the Far East. We were there on Coronation Day, when I stayed at home to look after the two boys, with a hired TV, while Alice joined a friend in a stand in London to watch the proceedings.

CHAPTER 10

RETURN TO THE FAR EAST

SOON AFTER THE Coronation, but before the Fleet Review which we missed, I and the family sailed from Southampton in the troopship "Dilwara". A six weeks voyage to Singapore, during which we made friends with several Army families and Andy, the delightful Commander Anderson who was joining HMS "Newcastle", as Executive Officer, in Korea. Steaming down the Red Sea with a following wind, both Simon and Philip got heat exhaustion and ended up in the sick bay packed in ice to reduce their very high temperatures. A worrying few days, but they both recovered quickly, thank God, and otherwise, the trip was uneventful.

The C-in-C's Offices were at Phoenix Park in Tanglin on the outskirts of the city and ten miles from the naval base. A long waiting list for a married quarter at the base and at that time, unlike the Army and RAF, there was no subsidised rental scheme. So we had to find rented accommodation in the city at the normal commercial rate. This was difficult to find and expensive. Meantime, we stayed at a boarding house in Nassim Road close to the Botanical Gardens. About a month later we moved into a modern second floor flat in Tanglin, but it quickly proved to be too cramped for two active children and we moved to an old house further out of town and close to a Malay Kampong (village). We had also found the professional Chinese Amah we had engaged unsatisfactory and changed to Malay servants. They were untrained but charming and delightful young people.

I should explain that in that hot and oppressive tropical climate and with no air conditioning at that time, one had to have servants. In that old house we also had an Indian cook and the kitchen was outside, separate from the house and very rudimentary.

Meantime, I settled down to my first proper shore job after nearly 14 years in the RN, apart from, of course, the periods when I was sick on shore. Amongst the C-in-C's large staff was an intelligence unit headed by CSO (1), a Captain, his Deputy, a Commander and three Desk Officers, two Lieutenant Commanders, and a Captain, Royal Marines. The Senior Lieutenant Commander covered the northern half of the Far East, the Royal Marine the southern, while I covered commercial maritime activity. I was also Staff Officer (Trade) responsible for planning naval control of shipping in the Far East. The latter was in its infancy but it led to an interesting experience. In early 1954, the United States C-in-C Pacific (Admiral Felix B Stump) convened a conference at Pearl Harbour to discuss the creation of an Allied Naval Control of shipping organisation in the Far East. He invited representatives from Singapore and Australia and my C-in-C responded by signal, nominating me. In due course, I flew from RAF Changhi to the US Clark Field near Manila. Here I was given a seat in a super constellation of the Military Air Transportation Service (MATS), a large organisation linking the US forces in Japan and Korea etc with the US. In a propeller driven plane, it was a long flight with three refuelling stops. At one of them, Kwajalein Island, where we landed at night, I was suddenly hauled off the plane and taken to a basement for questioning by security staff. They wanted to know who I was, what was my business and where were my 'orders'. The only 'orders' I had on me was a copy of the C-in-C's signal nominating me for the conference, and only after a lengthy wait did they eventually accept that I was a bona fide passenger! Here, I learned how regulated the US forces are, that everything has to be done by the book and that no serviceman can move without copious orders! This also became apparent at the conference, but it was an agreeable occasion and interesting too, as I was taken around Pearl Harbour, the famous Waikiki Beach and Diamond Point and incidentally, all the used car lots, which rather spoiled an otherwise beautiful place! After a final meeting with the famous Admiral Felix B Stump at the end of a successful week, I flew back to Manila as the sole passenger in a US Navy DC6.

Back on the domestic scene, we stayed at the old house for many months, during which we took some local leave up country in Malaya at Port Dickson where we rented a Government bungalow right on the beach. Because the climate in Singapore was so enervating and unhealthy, the Admiral required everyone to take 14 days station leave out of Singapore.

The wealthier officers caught passing troopships and went to Hong Kong. Too expensive for us and in any case, a beach holiday was far more suitable for small children. The climate was drier and sunnier and we felt refreshed. In Singapore we had joined the Tanglin Club which provided a lovely swimming pool, tennis and squash courts and a cinema on Sunday nights. We often used to take the boys for a swim on Sunday mornings with lunch at the pool side. We were also invited to attend a Malay wedding at the Kampong, where the bride and groom, both gorgeously dressed and made up, had to sit like statues for hours before the ceremony and subsequent celebrations took place. Our next move was to a very nice flat at Raffles college in the lovely grounds of Singapore University. As was traditional in those days, the European occupants were taking three months leave in Britain and this period fitted neatly before we became due for a married quarter at the naval base. Unfortunately, this got delayed for two or three months and left us with a problem. However, with no rent to pay, an RAF family we knew joined my family to spend a month in the Cameron Highlands up country at the Smoke House Inn! Built like an old English inn with log fires in the evenings, this was an ideal break from the enervating climate of Singapore. My RAF friend, who was Secretary of the Far East Joint Intelligence Committee, spent the first two weeks with the families and I spent the last two up there. Both wives incidentally were pregnant. On returning to Singapore, we spent the remaining weeks of waiting for our married quarter with old naval friends, Mike and Sylvia O'Leary, who were also waiting for their quarter.

Meanwhile I travelled daily to Phoenix Park to my job, which continued unchanged, watching Soviet Maritime Trade with Communist China, the latter's activities in the Formesa Straits and the growing Chinese merchant fleet, which necessitated the acquisition of some knowledge of Chinese dialects, e.g. Mandarin, Cantonese, etc, and the Chinese Telegraphic Code (CTC) with which baffled Europeans sought to understand and identify Chinese.

In November 1954, we moved into our married quarters at Rimau near the dockyard at the naval base. Typically, these houses had been flung up temporarily in the 1930's to house the staff building the naval base, but were still there to house us. Riddled with termites, they had to have extensive repairs between tenants (hence the delay) but nonetheless a godsend to poor Naval Officers after being forced to rent in the expensive Singapore housing market. Here, we employed a Chinese cook who was once in the RN and had a strong Pompey accent, and a very charming Chinese Amah. I had to drive nearly 10 miles to Phoenix Park, but life was easier and within our means. The other houses were occupied by our friends so social life was plentiful. There were also the occasional official parties to attend in Singapore, given by our C-in-C, Admiral Sir Charles Lambe, or Senior Intelligence Officers, etc. Our second CSO(1) was the redoubtable Captain Morgan Giles, who had a distinguished war record. He was married to an Australian millionairess and had a big family. He subsequently became a Rear Admiral and after retirement, MP for Winchester. They were very sociable. I also found time to play hockey in the C-in-C's team, which joined a local league, so there was a match every week. There were several Indian teams and the standard was high. Tennis too, at the Tanglin Club and I once played squash with Mike O'Leary, but in that climate, it was too much!

On the 18th February 1955 Alice gave birth to our daughter, Vivien, at the maternity hospital in Johore Bahru. This was over the Causeway and in Malaysia, but was actually the nearest hospital to the Naval base. It was staffed by highly qualified English Consultants and excellent nurses, so was a good place for Alice after 18 months in such a demanding climate. Life continued smoothly. Simon now 5, attended the dockyard school and the family could use the swimming pool in the barracks (FSA). Late that summer, when my time on the staff was drawing to an end, I was summoned by the Chief of Staff, Rear Admiral George Norfolk, who said I was to be recommended for a command. In recent promotion lists there had been a noticeable preponderance of promotions for First Lieutenants of the large 'Daring' class destroyers which were all commanded by Captains (with more influence than mere Commanders). So I asked if I could not go as First Lieutenant of a 'Daring'. "No!" said the Rear Admiral, "the C-in-C and I are certain that you are ideal for a command". Who can argue with that?

On 6th September 1955 we left the house at Rimau to embark in the troopship "Empire Orwell" after farewell visits from many friends and tears from Amah who had become really attached to the family. She was not a trained baby Amah, like the unsuitable Singapore Amahs and was quite different, showing emotions like us. Alice wrote to her later and I still have her charming reply. "Empire Orwell" was one of the better and faster troopships and we arrived at Southampton on 29th September after over two years abroad. I was entitled to over six weeks foreign service leave, but as we had sold the house in Rainham, the family had found a largish rented house only half a mile from theirs in Bexhill into which we moved. During our leave we house hunted unsuccessfully and I visited the Admiralty where I was told I would command the type 15 frigate "Verulam" for her trials after refit, after which I would be given my proper command.

CHAPTER 11

IN COMMAND

H MS "VERULAM" WAS at Barclay Curles yard on the Clyde and I arrived in Glasgow on 12th December 1955. However, the ship was not ready and I was put up in a boarding house in Glasgow. This was quite the coldest house I can ever remember and no amount of bedding, great coat, etc, kept me from shivering the nights away. During the day I visited the ship, met the officers and lunched with the dockyard manager and his staff to get a grip on the situation. I had not been in a civil dockyard since "Meteor's" refit at the Wallsend Slipway on the Tyne in 1943 and I was struck by the poor relationship between the management and the workers. The latter, be they shipwrights, welders, riveters or joiners, all skilled men, had a tough life, particularly in a Scottish winter, but I was told in a contemptuous way that, after payment on a Friday, most of the men would go straight to the pub outside the dock gates and their wives would be lucky to see any of that pay. Meanwhile, the management lunched well in their office block every day, courtesy of the Company. I wonder how much of the 'them and us' attitude caused the demise of most of the British shipbuilding industry.

On 4th January 1956 we commissioned and on the 9th sailed down the Clyde to start the trials. Up to this time, I had always served in ships with open bridges, with a good all round view, but the type 15's on conversion from 'V' class destroyers, had been fitted with the new style covered bridge, following the American pattern. I should also mention that whereas Captains and Commanders were invariably given courses prior to taking command, Lieutenant Commanders taking command of local flotilla ships in the home bases were not. So here I was, after 2½ years in a shore job and in a tropical climate, about to pilot my frigate down the Clyde from an unfamiliar bridge, on a freezing cold day in a thick fog! I stood on the bridge roof in my great coat with a gyro compass repeater and microphone to the Coxswain in the wheelhouse and conned the ship down the river to a buoy where we secured for compass swinging. After that I controlled the ship from the covered bridge. We spent several days at sea testing equipment, carrying out a full power trial and securing alongside at Gourock each night. But during a day at sea on 17th January for gunnery and radar trials, a full force 10 gale blew up. The weather was far too bad to berth alongside that evening, so I decided to secure to A1 buoy at the tail of the bank. Unfortunately, the weather overcame the whaler carrying the picking up wire, which disappeared into the darkness. Such was the weather that anchoring would have left us insecure for the night. The problem was accentuated by having far fewer seamen than normal, most of whom had disappeared in the whaler. So there was nothing for it but to try and lay the bows onto the windward side of the buoy long enough for the picking up wire to be hooked on. It must have taken at least half an hour, but eventually my very resourceful First Lieutenant David Joel, himself shinned down and secured the wire and then two bridles (cables) while I held the ship to the buoy. Much relief and we could all relax and have a good night in a typical howling Scottish gale. Although the trials had not been completed by 20th January, we were nonetheless ordered to pay off and I took the ship up the Gareloch and alongside the Reserve Fleet Depot ship "Woolwich" from where I returned to Bexhill to await my next appointment.

My first command had lasted only a few weeks but all the experience I had had in 5 previous destroyers and frigates stood me in good stead. Of course I lacked experience in ship handling but that came quickly. Like everyone, I made mistakes but happily none with any serious consequences. Ever since I was a young boy, I had always dreamed of commanding a destroyer and I felt happy and confident. My next command was the type 16 frigate "Termagant", attached to the 3rd Submarine Squadron and based at Rothesay in Scotland. I was very lucky because although both "Verulam" and "Termagant" were now classed as frigates, they were originally destroyers and retained their original steam turbine engines of 40,000hp driving twin screws. They were much easier to handle than, for example, the 'Castle' class single screw frigates or the later type 12's based at Portland and commanded by my contemporaries.

I joined "Termagant" at Devonport on 12th February 1956 and a few weeks later sailed for Rothesay. In the meantime however, Alice had found a suitable permanent home for us in a village called Northiam in East Sussex. On a weekend visit, I agreed with her choice and we bought it. Hard to believe but a 4 bedroomed cottage for £1,400 needing re-decorating but otherwise sound! We could not do anything about it then as I was due to sail for Rothesay and in early April, Alice left Bexhill to join me. After an initial stay in the Glenburn Hotel, we found a delightful semi-detached cottage, the other half being used by the lady owner at weekends, when she returned from her work at a Glasgow hospital. In those days, the 3rd Submarine Squadron with Captain S/M3 based in the Depot ship "Adamant" was basically training newly commissioned boats working up and the famous "Perishers" course for qualifying submarine Commanding Officers (COs). "Termagant" was primarily involved with the latter and we worked three terms a year with leave periods in between. "Termagant" was "home sea service" for my Devonport ship's company and since none had their families in Rothesay, where there were no married quarters anyway, it was not a popular draft. I was very aware of this and so continued my predecessor's practice of taking the ship to Devonport each leave period. This meant, of course, that for my own leave I either had to travel to Rothesay or the family had to come south. Over time, we did both.

For most of the time, we were at sea daily, providing a target for the "Perishers". Elementary attacks early in the term advancing to a major exercise at the end of term, when a Home Fleet destroyer squadron would come up to escort "Adamant" to sea as a major target. I, of course, was junior to all Home Fleet destroyer Commanders and so was tail end Charlie. Unlike them with their full complements, "Termagant" had a reduced ship's company and only a leading signalman rather than a Yeoman of signals. Fortunately, I had always enjoyed communications and found that I could still read manoeuvring flags or light signals as fast, or faster than him. An additional bit of fun was torpedo collection which was "Termagant's" responsibility, for which we were specially fitted with a derrick and storage racks instead of our usual torpedo tubes. On these big days the "Perishers" fired a salvo of 4 torpedoes with blowing heads so that, at the end of their run, they would float vertically, It was a point of honour to see how fast we could recover them and get back into station on the screen. The trick was to drift down on them and try and recover all four alongside, but much depended on wind and weather conditions, and sometimes we would have to lower the whaler. Other memories I have are of periscopes disappearing dangerously close under our bows, as the submarine went deep – with our hearts in our mouths, but we never hit them! Occasionally we would spend the night anchored off the isle of Arran with the submarine alongside and enjoy some mutual hospitality. Fortunately the "Perishers" had other things to do, such as the attack teacher in Rothesay or theoretical training in HMS "Dolphin" at Gosport, so the Staff Officer operations in "Adamant" could vary our routine. In May 1956, we paid an official visit to Belfast. This meant that, on our arrival, I had to don my sword and medals and pay official calls on the Belfast dignitaries from the Lord Mayor downwards. Fine people that they are, I found that Ulstermen don't find the social graces easy and invariably, after the first minute, a desk drawer would be opened and out would come a bottle of Bushmills Whisky and a couple of glasses! This eased the atmosphere perfectly. They enjoyed their return calls to the ship and apart from restrictions on where we could go in Belfast because of the 'Troubles', the visit went well.

In July 1956 it was the turn of Rothesay to host the Clyde Regatta, a major sailing occasion. Because "Adamant" was away on a NATO exercise in the West Indies, "Termagant" was appointed Guardship. At this point, I should mention that I was blessed with an excellent First Lieutenant John Hamilton, who always kept the ship immaculate. So much so, that the submariners used to call us their yacht, so I had no worries about the ship while I attended to the protocol and entertainment involved. This was considerable as the occasion was also graced by the presence of Prince Philip, Duke of Edinburgh and the Royal Yacht "Britannia". After the last race was started each day, I would cross the bay in my Skimmer, dressed with sword and medals, to join the starting committee with their champagne and canapés. Every evening each Yacht Club in turn would have a reception or dance to which Alice and I were invited. There was also a reception in "Britannia". At this and other times, we also saw a great deal of the Lord Lieutenant of Bute and his wife, Lord and Lady Crichton-Stuart, both elderly and he the uncle of the Marquis of Bute. A very charming couple who once asked Alice and I and the children to tea on a Sunday afternoon. A memorable occasion because he allowed Simon and Philip to charge around their large lawn in his electric invalid wheelchair, which they loved. The regatta lasted a fortnight and the entertainment seemed to go on forever but all good things come to an end and it was back to work with the "Perishers".

We went south for the summer leave that year, left the children with the family at Bexhill and went over daily to our cottage in Northiam, where we re-decorated the whole place in 10 days. Soon after returning to Rothesay – the family by train and I in "Termagant" from Devonport - we left for an official visit to Namsos in Norway. Namsos is about 100 miles north of Trondheim and a small town of wooden houses. During the abortive 1940 fighting it was totally destroyed as a result of which I understood that there was still a lot of anti-British feeling for having caused their misfortune. Namsos also had a Socialist Mayor and the town was dry – to the dismay of the ship's company! I called on the Mayor, who spoke no English, and the officers were entertained to dinner very formally with hosts and guests on opposite sides of a large table on which was placed one bottle of beer per person! Our return party led to our meeting a Norwegian Baron who lived on a hill overlooking the town and who owned large forestry interests. Such were the strict drink/driving laws that the Baron apologised profusely for refusing to drink any alcohol. He then invited a party of officers to dinner at his house the following night. And what a dinner and how the wine and Aquavit flowed! At the end of which I found myself conforming to the delightful Norwegian custom, where the principal guest makes a little "tak for Matem" speech. The visit went well and the ship's company behaved immaculately. It was clear that it was as much a diplomatic visit as a jolly for us. I was presented with two books about the Vikings and Namsos by the Mayor, which I still have and we left them a ship's badge.

Down south again for Christmas 1956 and the family came to Plymouth for a short time before we all returned to Rothesay again. At the end of the spring term we were joined by a Norwegian frigate, who took part in the "Perishers" exercises. One day her Captain came to lunch in "Termagant" and brought a bottle of Aquavit with him. The Commander (Submarines) (S/M) Ken Martin, also came and submariners are never frightened of some alcohol, so the whole bottle was consumed before lunch by the three of us! About this time, we also had our annual inspection by Captain S/M3 and his staff. The Captain was new, the famous one-eyed Ian McGeoch (later Vice-Admiral Sir Ian McGeoch). He had lost an eye when his submarine was sunk off Sicily and he became a Prisoner of War (POW). The inspection consisted of a harbour inspection of ship's company and ship, general and

GHG as a corporal in Cheltenham College OTC, 1938 (extreme right).

Cheltenham College Public School fencing champions, 1940.

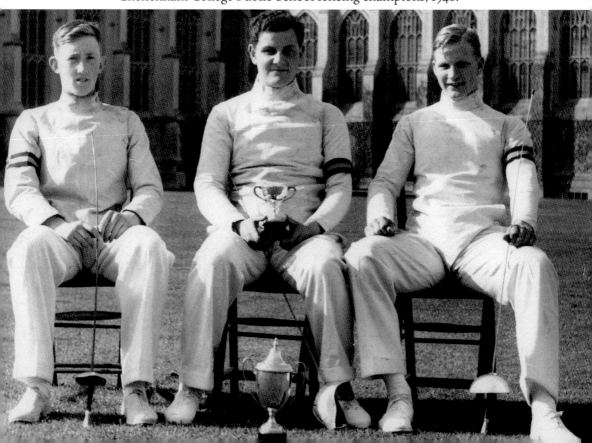

GHG in new cadet's uniform, with family, 1940.

HMS Danae.

HMS Vanoc.

HMS Goathland.

HMS Meteor.

1944. Russian convoy, *HMS Meteor* in foreground. Print of painting.

(Left) GHG at Devonport, 1944.

(Right) GHG at Malta, 1947.

HMS Newcastle, leaving Malta, with C-in-C Mediterranean.

Captain Doug Wright, RM, riding his motorcycle on my precious quarterdeck in 1948.

HMS Peacock leaving Malta, 1950.

HMS Peacock, 1950. Cartoon of ship's officers.

HMS *St Kitts*. The event that never happened!
(The King's 2nd tour to South Africa in *HMS
Vanguard*), 1952.

HMS *St Kitts* at
Gibraltar, 1952.

HMS *Termagant* 1956/57. In command at
Rothesay, Scotland.

GHG on promotion to Commander, 1958.

GHG at GHQ, ME Episkopi, Cyprus in 1959. Farewell to Admiral Miers.

St Vincent night dinner. Captain Fetherston-Dilke with Vice-Admiral Sir Raymond Hawkins, GHG, and Sir Peter Carey, 1965.

St Vincent night dinner. Captain Fetherston-Dilke with Admiral Sir Derek Holland-Martin and GHG, 1966.

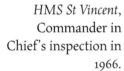

HMS St Vincent, Commander in Chief's inspection in 1966.

HMS St Vincent 1966. Senior Classes departing, led by the Royal Marine Band.

fire drill and then to sea for the operational inspection. All went well and we had a nice complimentary signal after what is a major ordeal. Sometime in the late spring of 1957, when we were lying at our buoy in Rothesay bay, the RFA oiler "Black Ranger" was coming alongside to fuel us, when her diesel engine failed to go astern and she hit us hard on the starboard quarter. We suffered a 10 foot gash from the upper deck down to just below the water line in, of all places, the wardroom wine store! Tugs came over from the Clyde and we were towed up there for repairs. But there was a Scottish shipyard strike going on and the Admiralty ordered us to be placed up the Gareloch alongside the Reserve Fleet depot ship "Woolwich". Here, naval shipwrights effected temporary repairs and as the Easter leave was due, we sailed for Devonport. Soon after our arrival, dockyard officials arrived on board and solemnly told us that repairs would not be possible for many weeks. This was dismaying as we were due to pay another visit to Norway after Easter, to say nothing of the summer training programme at Rothesay. When I took command of "Termagant" at Devonport early the previous year, I had called on the elderly Admiral Superintendent as was customary. Before leaving him he had said in a fatherly way that if I ever needed help or advice, I was not to hesitate to ask him. So I took him up on that, went to see him, explained the situation and asked for priority repairs. Within 24 hours, we were into dry dock and repairs underway! I went on leave a very happy man!

So we got our visit to Arendal, which is a largish port with a Master Mariners Club and quite different from Namsos, and arrived back at Rothesay in time for the summer programme. Later that summer, "Termagant" was ordered to Campbeltown to escort the new hydrogen peroxide driven submarine "Explorer" during her trials. The existence of this strange craft resulted from the capture at the end of the war, of the German experimental submarine "Meteorite". Hydrogen peroxide (HB) is a very powerful fuel and high underwater speeds can be achieved. But it is also extremely volatile and the slightest dirt or foreign body can cause it to explode. Consequently, the crew were living ashore and HP bags were fixed outside the pressure hull. This dangerous craft was commanded by Lance Bell-Davies, whose father had been a World War I Naval VC. His son was delightful and in the same mould. Approaching the jetty at Campbeltown was one of the only two occasions when I had to ring down 'full astern' as I suddenly realised that we were not going to stop in time! It was low tide and

I had failed to realise that we were suffering from 'shallow water effect' when the propellers don't grip the water properly. After various preliminary trials the day came for the full power trial which was to be for three hours down the deep St Georges' channel between Scotland and Northern Ireland. This was because no one knew what would happen to the control of a submarine doing the expected 30 knots, faster than any submarine had ever gone at that time (the nuclears came later). Because, at that speed, "Termagant's" sonar and underwater telephone (with which we were specially fitted) would be useless, Lance and I arranged a series of white candles to be fired by "Explorer" and to be measured by me from abeam. Unfortunately "Explorer's" acceleration left "Termagant" astern and even going flat out at over 30 knots, we could only keep about ½ mile astern of "Explorer". So the speed measurement had to be approximate but was clearly over 30 knots, a world record at the time. Towards the end of the run we were startled to see a red grenade come up from "Explorer" the sign for an emergency, and shortly after she surfaced. It is extremely difficult for a ship like "Termagant" with high pressure steam turbines to stop that quickly but we managed it with our boiler safety valves lifting and making a deafening noise. It turned out that "Explorer" had suffered another bag explosion, a frightening experience, but no serious harm done and in all other respects, a brilliant performance. Sadly, HP driven Submarines were not developed as nuclear propulsion was safer and more practical.

One of the most important duties of Naval Officers is to get to know all the ratings under their command and to monitor their progress in the Navy. Some may remain AB's, others may attain Leading rate or become Petty Officers and, in due course, Chief Petty Officers. More rarely, one may find an outstanding young rating who is potentially suitable for commissioned rank, i.e. to become an officer. In "Termagant", such a one was the Stores Petty Officer, who was young, bright, efficient and with a pleasant personality. I started what were known as CW Papers for him. Of course we went our separate ways and I never knew what happened to him until years later, one of my sons who followed me in to the Navy, joined a frigate as a sub Lieutenant and found that the Supply Officer was this very man. That gave me enormous pleasure. It illustrates the huge responsibility Officers have and how they can influence the lives of others.

During that summer, we were informed of forthcoming major changes. The 3rd Submarine Squadron was to leave Rothesay and move to the

Gareloch where the Reserve Fleet had been run down. At the same time, "Termagant" was to be paid off and relieved by a type 12 frigate from Portland. So at the end of the big summer term exercise, amid a flurry of very complimentary signals about our service to the 3rd Submarine Squadron, we bade farewell and sailed for Devonport to pay off. I had only had 20 months in command but, as I hope I have shown, it was full of events and interest and dare I say it, the best Command in home waters for a Lieutenant Commander.

I was appointed First Lieutenant of Portsmouth barracks but before joining there, I was sent on two temporary appointments. In early October 1957 I took command of HMS "Tumult", another type 16 frigate, at Chatham for trials. These were briefer than those for "Verulam" two years earlier but I suffered the same shortage of officers and men and remember a somewhat hairy passage down the Medway and into the Thames Estuary without a navigator. However, my two years in command got me through and I returned "Tumult" to Chatham Dockyard in one piece. I was then appointed in November to join a tactical investigation at the RN Tactical School at Woolwich. Here I joined a large team of destroyer, frigate and submarine Commanding officers, many of them old friends. We were to fight a theoretical battle of the Atlantic 1965, with the weapons with which it was anticipated that the Russians and ourselves would be equipped by that time. The Tactical School was equipped with a master tactical table surrounded by cubicles, each representing a destroyer, frigate or submarine. Each of us was confined to his cubicle and took individual action to meet the circumstances we were confronted with. The investigation was of sufficient importance to receive visits from the Admiralty, including the then First Lord of the Admiralty, Mr Soames. One conclusion of the investigation was that the very large convoy still represented the best defence against the growing Soviet submarine and nuclear threat.

Throughout this period, from August 1957, when I paid off "Termagant", to December when I finally became First Lieutenant of RN barracks Portsmouth, the family moved into our cottage at Northiam and we thanked God that we had this roof over our heads. Not long after our arrival, my wife remarked to me what a change it would be to be away from the Navy. She had accompanied me from Portsmouth in 1947 to Malta, then to Chatham, to Singapore and finally to Rothesay in almost exactly 10 years. The following morning, there was a knock at the front door and standing there was none other than Captain John Frewen, Royal Navy, (later Admiral Sir John Frewen) who was then commanding the Aircraft Carrier "Eagle", and who, like me, happened to be home for the weekend. He lived right opposite us and was in effect the Squire of the village, where his family had lived for a very long time. The family estate and its fine Tudor mansion had been turned into a school. Was there no escape from the Navy? We need not have worried, as although I heard that 'Black Jack' Frewen, as he was known in the service, was a bit of a terror, in the village he was charm himself and we got on very well. On 21st September, when again I happened to be home, our fourth child Christina was born. The village GP happened to be away as was the local district Nurse, but the locum nurse who came was excellent and Tina was born without trouble and with me providing assistance: the first time I was actually present at the birth of any of my children. Such circumstances would be rare nowadays as even Naval Officers are given leave from wherever they are, to attend their children's births.

CHAPTER 12

PROMOTION

WHEN I JOINED RN Barracks (RNB) Portsmouth in early December 1957, the family remained at the cottage and it was just as well we had made no further arrangements, as on 31st December 1957 my name appeared on the list of promotions to Commander! It was apparent that my time in command had borne fruit and perhaps if I had gone as First Lieutenant of a "Daring" I would not have made it. Promotions were provisional for 6 months and would be confirmed on 30th June 1958. Meanwhile I had to keep my nose clean! Promotion did solve one problem. The Navy was being reduced in size as officer strength had been swollen when many wartime officers were given permanent commissions after the war. This was leading to an increase in competition for the reduced numbers being promoted, so a reduction was welcome. They had introduced what had become known as 'The Golden Bowler scheme' – a financial inducement to take early retirement. The thought of being a 'passed over' Lieutenant Commander for the next 15 years until reaching normal retirement age did not appeal to me and so I applied for scheme B – retirement if not promoted. With my growing family, promotion left me in little doubt that I should continue to serve, to which, I might add that I never had any regrets about joining a service for which I had tremendous respect and loyalty. There was however, one little doubt which I shall explain later, and which required some thought.

As a result of promotion, I remained at RNB Portsmouth for only three months and was then appointed to the RN staff course at Greenwich, which I joined in mid March 1958. Whereas the Army and RAF staff courses lasted a year and were vital for career and promotion, the Naval staff course lasted only six months and was taken less seriously. Nevertheless, I had been conscious for a long time that my shortened war time training as a cadet, Midshipman and acting Sub Lieutenant left a lot to be desired and had applied to do the staff course while serving in "St Kitts". So I got my wish and was not disappointed. For a start, the routine allowed me to spend three nights a week, Friday to Sunday, at home. We started work at Greenwich mid-morning on Mondays and finished at lunch time on Fridays. During that period you were expected to live in at Greenwich and work like hell! And we did! The course was a mixture of basic staff work methodology, individual essays, group schemes, presentations to your fellow students, and to hear at least two lectures a day. These lectures were given by top class people – Government ministers, Trade Union leaders and experts in many fields, so that one developed a knowledge of how the country was run and how the armed forces were run by Government. We also had fascinating day visits to places such as Lloyds of London, the Ford Motor factory and Smithfield Market etc, to see how the other half lived and worked. Last but not least, we spent an exchange week at the RAF Staff college at Bracknell. Here we were confronted by a thoroughly brain washed crowd who believed passionately that the V-bomber force should be the only provider of the strategic nuclear deterrent, just when the arrival of nuclear submarines looked like providing a better future alternative! The debate raged furiously, but we still found time to play a golf match at Wentworth! The ethos at Bracknell was very different to Greenwich. Here they had spacious grounds, married quarters for all and even their own golf course. They were all very serious and had to pass an exam at the end of their year. Failure ruined their career.

During the staff course, we were invited to visit our Appointers at the Admiralty to discuss our future careers. Since 1956, the promotion lists to Commander had been split into post and general lists because there were now insufficient sea commands for all and many staff appointments, both national and NATO, etc. These rapidly became christened "Wet and Dry" lists, and I had appeared on the "Dry" list. Since I had spent practically all my career so far at sea, I found this selection somewhat odd and disappointing. So, another newly promoted "salt horse" and I went up to the Admiralty in high dudgeon to see our Appointer. A 'Salt Horse' by the way was a Seaman Officer who had not specialized in e.g. Gunnery, Navigation, Signals etc and tended to serve in Destroyers or frigates or other small ships. We were told that because we had so much sea time, we had to make way for

Aviators and Submariners who lacked time at sea in surface ships. Much later, I realised that the underlying reason was to ensure that those destined for the top, the so called 'flyers', got the necessary sea commands. Nevertheless, to get one's brass hat was the major promotion and one became a senior officer, and there were good and interesting jobs to be had. So again, with the family in mind, I resolved to continue serving. As far as future appointments were concerned, I expressed an interest in intelligence and, in due course, I was selected to be Staff Officer (Intelligence) Middle East. Although intelligence achieved some fame in World War I, through Room 40, intelligence was in fact unfashionable in the modern Navy and not for ambitious officers. However, because of my interest in modern history and current affairs, (including my entry exam marks) I felt that I had a flair for it and would enjoy it.

CHAPTER 13

BACK TO INTELLIGENCE
ON THE DRY LIST

O N COMPLETION OF the staff course, home leave, and a briefing in the Admiralty Naval Intelligence Division. I flew to Cyprus in September 1958. During the long slow flight in a DC4 I read a paperback entitled "A History of the Arabs" to give me some sort of grasp of the complexities of the Middle East. I had also read T E Lawrence's "Seven Pillars of Wisdom" so was not entirely ignorant.

My boss, the new CSO(1) Med, was Captain Gregory-Smith. He had elected to station himself with the C-in-C in Malta, so I actually relieved the old CSO(1) in Cyprus. Apart from being CSO(1)'s deputy, I was also the naval member of the JIC (ME) and on the staff of the Flag Officer Middle East. He was the famous submarine VC Rear Admiral Miers. An irascible and hard man to serve. I quickly became aware of his dislike of intelligence, but in fact, this was entirely due to the previous CSO(1) who had told the Admiral quite untruly, that there were intelligence matters he, the Admiral, could not see. I resolved this one morning by taking down to the Admiral a huge pile of signals and reports, which comprised the previous days "take" and explained to him that though he could see any or all of this raw material, it was my task to sift and analyse it all and then report to him, the C-in-C in Malta and the Admiralty in London. I never had another squeak out of him. The biggest problem in Cyprus at that time was the fact that 30,000 British troops were battling the serious revolt by the so called Colonel Grivas who sought 'Enosis', or union with Greece. This was quite unacceptable to the large Turkish minority and hence to the British Government. The emergency led to a ban on Service families coming to the island and so Alice and the family had to remain at home in Northiam. So I lived in the Senior Officer's Mess in GHQ Middle East, at Episkopi, with Army officers from Lieutenant colonel to Brigadier in rank. RAF Senior Officers lived at the nearby RAF base at Akrotiri. I had a Sudanese servant and lived comfortably. We worked what in the Navy we called tropical routine – 0700-1300, then finish for the day, but in my case, I used to wander up to the office between 1700 and 1800 and do another hour's work. In the afternoon I played tennis or hockey. I was Captain of the local Navy hockey team – so got very fit. The monotony of office life was broken by trips around my parish. I flew to Malta to see my boss, CSO(1), to Kuwait and Bahrain in the Persian Gulf and to the Lebanon, where there was a Naval attaché and where M16 had their regional HQ. When leaving on these trips, I had to travel from Episkopi to Nicosia with an armed escort of two Royal Marines, as the Greek rebels were making life extremely dangerous outside the military bases. In those days, when serving abroad, one was entitled to 14 days station leave (and 2 days per month abroad Foreign Service leave on return to the UK). On two occasions and after great difficulty, I managed to get what were called "indulgence flights" in RAF aircraft flying to the UK. One had to wait weeks and was suddenly given 24 hours notice, so I had to return to Cyprus via BEA at my own expense to make sure I returned on time. One RAF flight was in a Beverly transport, sitting in the enormous transport deck, flying at 120 mph and stopping at El Adem in North Africa, Malta and Marseilles and taking two days.

After about a year and with the emergency situation easing, families were once again allowed to join their husbands in Cyprus. I had been on the waiting list for a married quarter (living outside the base was still too risky), but my list was not only for Lieutenant Colonels (my equivalent) but also Colonels and Brigadiers. To my dismay, I discovered that because the more senior officers scored more points, I was going down not up the list, and my prospects began to look bleak and hopeless. Fortunately, the Admiralty ran a scheme whereby if you were abroad without your family, you need only serve 18 months in the appointment. And so it was that I was relieved in February 1960 and returned home. In many ways this was a pity, as I found the job fascinating and enjoyable. At that time, it was all very secret, but the existence of the Sigint Station in Cyprus is now well known. Its principal target was military activity in the Southern Soviet Union, but it also had an Arab section. At that time Colonel Nasser was establishing and endeavouring to increase his power in the Middle East following the Suez Crisis in 1956, and we were privy to much of the plotting and underhand activities that were characteristic of him. King Hussein and Colonel Kasim the Dictator of Iraq, where the young King Fiesel had been murdered, were his principal targets. There were also plenty of diplomatic and MI6 reports and I dispatched almost daily, lengthy signals to Malta and the Admiralty to keep them in touch with events. I was also the Naval member of the JIC (Middle East), the other members representing the Army, RAF, MI6, GCHQ and JIB, presided over by the Political Representative who was a Diplomat. We met and produced a weekly report. At any rate, it was nice to know that one's efforts were appreciated as I had compliments from both CSO(1) and Admiral Bingley, the C-in-C in Malta before leaving the job. Also before leaving Cyprus, I was told by my Appointer that I was being nominated to go as SOO to Flag Officer Scotland at Potreavie near Rosyth. This was the first time (but not the last) when I was faced with the well known conflict between career and family. The job would have been fine, but Scotland again, after so recently serving there in "Verulam" and "Termagant"? And just as the two boys were settled at prep school in Sussex! I explained the situation to the Appointer, emphasizing the point that one would perform better if the domestic situation was right. Mercifully, he saw the point and kindly changed the appointment.

Soon after my return from Cyprus, Alice said that she had met a family near Ewhurst about 2 miles from Northiam, who lived in a lovely old Tudor farmhouse. They were about to sell and move to Ireland, and would love us to buy it. We met, agreed a price and bought it! At £3,800 I wondered if we could afford it! But our cottage sold for £3,000 to the well known artist Frank Beresford, so the difference was not too formidable. However, during the next year we built a new kitchen and one day, when the local builder was still with us, he came up to me and asked if I realised that the floor at the end of the house was about to fall into the cellar! An RSJ had to be fitted and I began to learn that with old houses, your hand is never out of your pocket. Nevertheless, the house, which had 6 bedrooms and was in 2 acres of garden and woodland, was quite idyllic and ideal for a large family.

In March 1960, I joined the Joint Planning Staff (JPS) at the old Ministry of Defence at Storeys Gate in Parliament Square, London, and for the next 2½ years commuted daily from Sussex. The JPS consisted of teams of officers; one from each service, dealing with different aspects of national military planning and responsible through Deputy Directors to Directors at Captain RN/Colonel level. I found myself in the NATO team with a charming Army Major (who later commanded the Leicestershire regiment) and a senior Wing Commander. At this time Mr MacNamara, the US Secretary of Defence, had recommended a new NATO strategy of "nuclear flexible response" to a Soviet attack on the West as a solution to the problems associated with a total strategic nuclear response, which was increasingly regarded as unrealistic. I also had to deal with an Admiralty paper on 'the principals of NATO maritime strategy'. However, on 1st November 1961, I was suddenly transferred on a temporary basis, as Staff Officer to Field Marshall Festing. Following his retirement as Chief of the General Staff, Frankie Festing had been retained by the Defence Secretary, Mr Watkinson, to examine a new strategy prepared by the Chiefs of Staff, to draft the 1962 defence White Paper and to look at some other problems including the future of a new RAF aircraft, the TSR2. Three 2-star officers were appointed to assist the great man; a senior Civil Servant, an Air Vice Marshal and a Rear Admiral, who was Hill-Norton (later to become the First Sea Lord, then CDS and finally a Life Peer!) Belatedly, it was realised that they had no supporting staff and so I was hauled out of the JPS to fill this gap. Finally, a RAF Corporal Clerk was found to do the typing. The routine went like this: the three wise men would meet Frankie on a Thursday and decide on the following week's programme. The Field Marshal, who incidentally was a huge man who had a special chair made in the War Office to fit him, would catch the night train to Newcastle and to his estate, not to reappear until the following Tuesday. The three wise men would spend all day discussing aspects of the problems we had been given, with me sitting at the end of the table listening and taking notes. Just before 5pm without fail they would rise and depart, telling me to have a draft of whatever had been discussed, first thing the following morning. I worked late, and, for the first and only time in my life, would take the work, catch a late and partly empty train, find a secluded table in the buffet car and work on. The next morning the draft would be typed by the RAF Corporal ready to be handed to the three wise men when they arrived at about 10am. In mid-week there would be meetings and discussions with the Field Marshal and on two occasions, I remember accompanying him when he met the Chief of Defence Staff Lord Mountbatten. Just the two of them, with me sitting in a corner taking notes. It was certainly life at high pressure, but absolutely fascinating. In about 3 months, the new strategy was agreed and a draft White Paper prepared. The Festing team also recommended that the TSR2 project should be abandoned. In hindsight this was probably a major error as I often heard later that the TSR2 was years ahead of its time and could have been a huge success. The decision was pushed hard by Rear Admiral Hill-Norton, who was the strong and forceful member of the team. He was not Fleet Air Arm but had recently commanded the "Ark Royal" so perhaps he thought he knew all about aircraft! In January 1962, after about 3 months, the First Sea Lord wrote to the Field Marshal asking if he could return me to the JPS where I was needed. The team was, in any case, breaking up and so my time in this quite unique situation came to an end. Rear Admiral Hill-Norton, who was a grim and gruff man, graciously wrote to the Director of Plans and my Appointer a very flattering letter about my performance.

Just before I returned to the JPS in January 1962, Alice gave birth at home to our fifth child Ben, but then developed a deep thrombosis and was rushed to hospital, accompanied by Ben. No sooner was this sorted out and she returned home, when, at a month old, Ben developed a restriction called a "Pyloric Stenosis". So it was back to hospital where Ben had a small operation to free the restriction, which was very successful. All was well after that and after 2½ years, my time on the JPS came to an end in September 1962.

CHAPTER 14

TO CANADA

BY THAT TIME, I had happily accepted an appointment of two years exchange service with the Royal Canadian Navy. The family would accompany me, although we decided that our two eldest sons, then aged 13 and 11 respectively, should continue their education in the UK. Simon was about to go to Cheltenham College and Philip would remain in prep school at Hastings. Some very good friends undertook to look after them during the Easter holidays and as necessary, while they would join us by air for the summer and Christmas holidays. Meanwhile the autumn was busy with packing and arranging to let the house. Most of this went well, but as so often happens, we did experience two disasters. The packers, who came to collect our belongings for dispatch to Canada, loosely packed our china and glass, promising to repack them properly before departing to Canada. They did not do so, and when we opened the case at Ottawa, it was full of broken china and glass.

We thought we had found a tenant for the house, the Superintendent of a Mental Hospital in Glasgow, who wished to retire to live in Sussex, and wanted to rent while searching for somewhere to live. But as the date of our departure loomed nearer and no firm letting arrangements made, we began to worry. Just before we left we heard, to our horror, that the poor man had become a patient in his own asylum! Fortunately our farmer neighbours, who were related to the family we had bought the house from, offered to keep an eye on the house. Just as well, as within weeks of our leaving, the first snow of the famous winter 1962-63 arrived and continued throughout the winter. The ancient clay peg roof tiles had no lining and the farmer and his cowman ended up shovelling 18 inches of snow out of our very large attic! There is no doubt that they saved our house from ruin and a year later, we were able to let the house, through a local Estate Agent, to a quantity surveyor and his family. But, just 3 months before our return and their departure, they stopped paying the rent. The agent did nothing about it and on our return, my solicitor advised us not to throw good money after bad in pursuing the matter! I also discovered that they had left debts in the village, which made us feel awful. Such are the vicissitudes of letting property.

Meanwhile, we sailed from Liverpool in the Canadian Pacific liner "Empress of Canada" as First Class passengers, which should have been fun, but being November, we ran into a gale and had an extremely rough Atlantic crossing. The family were all laid up very seasick and I remember sitting in solitary state in the First Class dining room, enjoying the most delicious food! The passage up the St Lawrence Seaway was of course better, and we berthed at Montreal.

I was to be Assistant Director of Manning at the Canadian Naval Headquarters in Ottawa and we had agreed to take over my predecessor's rented house in the residential district called Rockcliffe. While he and his wife were packing up, he put us in a hotel apartment in Ottawa and I can still remember how grey and horrible Ottawa can be in November – very cold and dreary before the snow came. While there, we found and bought a lovely old Plymouth car, one lady owner and in perfect condition. In due course, we moved into the house at Rockcliffe, having bought the furniture from my predecessor. The district was where most of the diplomats and wealthier citizens lived and we discovered that our predecessors led a very social life. After a few months, the lease became due for renewal and we decided to move. We found a 50 year old house (which is old by Canadian standards) out beyond the town of Hull opposite Ottawa on the other side of the Ottawa River, and close to the Gatineau Park in Quebec Province. The house had 80 acres of land, mostly rough country, but in a beautiful location and several miles along a country lane. It was owned by a retired Canadian Army Colonel and his wife, with whom we got on very well. The delightful postal address was simply RR2, Aylmer, Quebec (RR2 meaning Rural Road No2). It was about 10 miles from the office in Ottawa and I quickly got used to the drive, even in the winter snow, as the roads were always cleared and treated very efficiently. The two girls now aged seven and five years, went to a state school in Aylmer, courtesy of a yellow school bus.

My job took me some time to get used to but the Canadians were pleasant and tolerant of this "Brit", particularly my boss, Captain Peter Cossette, who had trained in the UK and had an English wife. The Directorate was responsible for the manning of the two fleets on the East and West coasts, but this was complicated by a recent complete change in the trade structure of the personnel and the fact that there were insufficient men to man the existing fleet in a peacetime manner. There was a Nova Scotian civil servant who was a statistician and ran a punch card system recording every man, and who worked closely with me. There were junior officers supervising the new trade systems and long term planning. Each of the two fleets had a personnel depot commanded by a Commander, with whom I liaised closely. Herb Smith at Halifax was an interesting fellow with a typical Canadian background. Born and brought up on a farm on the prairies, he related to me how, in the fall (autumn) he and his brother would accompany their father with their horse and cart to a coal mine two days journey away. There, they would fill the cart with coal for the winter and journey two days back home. One day, when he was about 16, his father said "Son, you are joining the Navy" and took him to the railroad from where he travelled west to Esquimalt, the naval base on Vancouver Island, starting as a boy seaman. Herb was now a Commander and in his spare time was rebuilding an old Newfoundland Schooner. Later, when he retired, he took the schooner chartering in the West Indies. I flew several times to each coast to discuss the manning problems. At Halifax, I was told that if the Flag Officer saw a frigate alongside without good reason, he would order it to sea. Nor surprisingly, the married senior ratings resented this in peacetime and were leaving the Navy in droves. This was my problem.

When I took over, Peter Cossette kindly said that I was to take the same leave as the RCN, which was 30 days annually instead of the 14 days station leave allowed by the RN. By saving this up, we were able to enjoy lengthy tours in the United States in the summers of 1963 and 64. In 1963, we rented a cottage on the beach at Kennebunkport in Maine and with Simon and Philip joining us from school in the UK, the seven of us and our dog, toured gently through Vermont, New Hampshire and Maine, making stops on the way. We quickly discovered that Howard Johnson Motels were the most suitable for a large family as we could, for $16 a night, rent a large room with two king sized beds and a cot for Ben, plus camp beds we brought with us for the boys. Equally important, Howard Johnson always had a restaurant nearby where we could either have a meal or purchase take away food. From the cottage, one literally stepped out onto a large and beautiful sandy beach and the sea, although cold, was rough enough for some amateurish surfing. After our holiday there, we drove down to Boston to see the city and to investigate a distant relative. My maternal grandmother was a Blackstone and the first English settler who occupied what is now the Common in Boston, was the Reverend Blackstone. We found his statue and mention of him in Boston's history, but he eventually sold his land to other settlers, who were living in the more unhealthy swamp land surrounding Boston, and he moved to Providence, Rhode Island, where he died. We returned to Ottawa through New England by a different route and late enough to see the early fall colours in Massachusetts, New York State and Southern Ontario. A memorable holiday. The fall colours were equally gorgeous in our own garden, where we also witnessed the spectacular migration of thousands of birds to the south for the winter and north in the spring. The garden would suddenly be alive with birds in brilliant colours, who would rest for a few hours and then vanish as suddenly as they arrived. During the winter, we enjoyed the company of black Siberian squirrels, chipmunks and the occasional raccoon. The raccoons were unfortunately prone to rabies and one had to inform the police when one appeared in the garden. On one occasion, the poor animal clearly had rabies and had to be shot.

During the winter of 1962, I started skiing at Camp Fortune where the RCN ran a school on Saturday mornings. It was only 10 minutes away by car and I used a pair of old skis given to me by Admiral Wright, to whom I had had an introduction from Oliver Stirling-Lee. At the age of 41, I was never going to be a great skier and Camp Fortune was not an ideal place to learn. I can still remember standing in the class with a howling wind blowing around our ears and the temperature somewhere around minus 20°F. At some stage, Vivien started skiing, but Tina and Ben were too young. When Simon and Philip flew out for Christmas holidays, they joined me on the ski slopes and proved to be quick learners. On one memorable occasion, while on the slopes, we became aware that the snow which was falling had turned to frozen rain and the surface was becoming icy. So we stopped skiing and made our way to the car. By this time, the car was covered all over in a sheet of ice and we had some difficulty in gaining access and cleaning the windscreen. We then found that the roads were also a sheet of ice. We should have walked home, but I became determined to get the car home and with the invaluable help of the boys, we managed to push, shove and drive it home in about two hours – not the usual ten minutes. These weather conditions occur occasionally in central Canada and the ice builds up not only on the roads, but also on the power lines. On one occasion, many power lines were brought down in Montreal, leading to lengthy power failures. The traffic of course, is also brought to a standstill.

In July 1964, Alice went to the Ottawa General Hospital where she gave birth to Richard, our 6th child. They had not been back home long when our second summer trip to the USA was due. Sometime in late 1963, we received a letter from our tenant at Sempstead to say that an American doctor and his wife named Faulconer had visited, because his father had been born in Sempstead and his grandfather buried in Ewhurst churchyard. They were told that we were in Canada, but they were anxious to make contact. I immediately wrote to them at their home in Norfolk, Virginia, and in due course, correspondence developed leading to an invitation to stay with them next summer at their rented house at Virginia Beach. Despite being told the size of our family and the fact that they themselves had 4 children, they insisted that we should stay with them! And so our second long summer leave in the United States was settled around this visit. In early August, we left Canada in a large Ford estate which we had exchanged for our original car, the lovely old Plymouth, and drove south through New York State, Pennsylvania, Delaware, and Maryland and finally over the magnificent bridge across the mouth of Chesapeake Bay to Virginia Beach. There we stayed for a week with our charming hosts, Robin and Bunny Faulconer and their family. It transpired that during their several visits to the UK, they had visited the archives at Lewes, purchased books on the history of East Sussex and knew far more about our home than we did! Bunny was the daughter of a professor at the William and Mary University at Williamsburg and was highly educated, while Robin had qualified in medicine at the John Hopkins Hospital at Baltimore and was a Pathologist. We also met Robin's father and mother who lived in nearby Hampton and close to the Navy shipyard where he had worked after emigrating from the UK. They remained firm and close friends from this visit on. Following our week with the Faulconers, we headed west visiting first Williamsburg, the early capital of Virginia and now fully restored to its original state with even the guides dressed in 16th century clothes and allegedly speaking 16th century English! On westwards from there to Charlottesville where we visited Monticello, the famous home of Thomas Jefferson, the 3rd President of the USA. Jefferson was a man of many parts and designed his own home. His only error was to leave insufficient height for the weight of his long case clock, so he bored a hole in the floor to solve the problem. Curiously, both he and Washington, who signed the declaration of rights declaring that "all men are created equal" had slaves to run their estates. From there we drove northwards up the Blue Ridge Mountains to Washington. We visited the White House, Congress, the Smithsonian Institute, and Washington's home at Mount Vernon and then it was on to New York. Here we stayed in a large room in the Holiday Inn on 59th Street and visited Times Square, Wall Street and nearby Central Park. My clearest memory however is of Vivien now aged 9, suddenly learning to do the crawl in the swimming pool on the roof of the hotel! From New York, we headed north up the Hudson River, stopping at Lake George and once again witnessing the glorious fall scenery in the Adirondeck Mountains as we made our way back to Canada.

During the course of 1964, the Canadian armed forces faced a difficult situation with the proposal by Mr Hellyer, the Defence Minister, to amalgamate all three services into one with a single green uniform. It sounds ridiculous and led to sarcastic remarks that, for example a lieutenant in a frigate would be driving a tank in his next job and flying a fighter in the one after that! What Mr Hellyer envisaged was unclear but he forced his order through. In the RCN, nearly all the Admirals resigned and of more concern to me, my boss, Captain Peter Cossette, was called away to run some committee and I was officially appointed Director of Manning. This was a unique honour for a "Brit" and indicated the trust the Canadians had in me. However, it did not mitigate the manning problems we were struggling with and further representations were made to the Navy Board. Late in the year and shortly before I was due to be relieved, the Board relented. But instead of a gradual reduction in commitments, in typical Canadian fashion, they decided to pay off 15 "Prestonian" class World War II frigates in one go. I was not around to witness the ensuing manning chaos! Later, I heard from many sources how disliked the green uniform regime was and the Canadian forces fell into the doldrums. The single service was finally abandoned and the reputation of each of their services has, I believe, now recovered to what it always used to be.

Our two years in Canada sadly ended in November 1964. We had a great send off from Ottawa to Montreal by train, where we joined the Cunard liner "Carmania" for passage home. Another extremely rough trip. Sometime before our departure, we had heard from our tenant at Sempstead that the fabric of the house was in urgent need of repair. I had been warned that once again, I might receive an appointment up north but eventually was appointed as Executive Officer of HMS "St Vincent", the boys training establishment at Gosport. This was as good as you can get. I was extremely fortunate and was to join on 14th January 1965.

CHAPTER 15

PASSED OVER

MEANTIME, DURING MY Foreign Service leave, we started planning restoration work at Sempstead. Fortunately, I had been left a legacy and so had some resources for this. But this was interrupted by the serious illness of our youngest child, Richard, who at about 5 months old, was found to have Leukaemia. There followed weeks of treatment in and out of hospital, which naturally occupied the whole attention of Alice. I went off to Gosport and took over as Executive Officer at "St Vincent". The elder boys were away at public school and the younger three went to a local day school. Twice during my first term, St Helen's Hospital at Hastings telephoned to inform me that Richard had not long to live and advised my presence. I had a very capable Training Officer, who could run the establishment in my absence, but the Captain seemed insensitive to the situation and was very reluctant to let me go. Thanks to the devoted attention of the hospital staff, Richard survived through to the Easter leave when I was at home and he died then at the age of 9 months. Despite having five living and healthy children, Alice never got over the loss of Richard, but devoted her attention to the work at her beloved Sempstead. This started with the stripping of the very large roof, lining it, repairing the main chimney and relaying the tiles. Once or twice Alice and the family came to "St Vincent" and stayed at Cedar Cottage, the tied house that went with my job, but because of the schooling situation and repairs to Sempstead, it was never possible for the family to join me permanently. "St Vincent" ran in terms, like a school, so while it was difficult for me to get away during term time, I did have over six weeks leave a year.

The Executive Officer of a Naval ship or establishment is second in command and responsible to his Captain for the administration and discipline. However a training establishment is different in that it also has a complex and busy routine, starting with daily divisions on the Parade Ground and then classes, gymnasium and games, activities, etc, lasting all day. There were nearly 1,000 15 year old boys who were there for a year and divided into four divisions each supervised by a Lieutenant and divided into classes under CPO's or PO's. I was also President of the Wardroom with a large number of Officers, including Instructor Officers for the school and other specialists in a supporting role. The Wardroom had official dinners at least once a month and on 14th February, the anniversary of the Battle of Cape St Vincent, a very special dinner, to which a member of the board of Admiralty was invited. The boys were dressed in 19th century uniforms and there was much ceremonial formality and speeches. I also found myself, at the age of 45, playing hockey and tennis in the "St Vincent" teams. Once a month, there was a Commanders' lunch when the Executive Officers of the eight other establishments that then existed in the Portsmouth area, got together, hosted by each in turn. I had an office staff including a secretary, who was Gaye Hans-Hamilton, my predecessor's daughter, who amongst other things produced the daily orders.

During my first year the Captain and Training Officer were summoned to the Ministry of Defence on several occasions to plan a major change in new entry training. Because the state school leaving age had gone up to 16, the Navy had to cease recruiting 15 year old boys and to recruit from 16 years old upwards. Whereas the 15 year olds were given a year in a regime not unlike a public school, the adult entries were to receive only a 6 week new entry course before moving on to the specialist schools for part II training. "St Vincent" was to make the first radical change and for months thereafter, the Training Officer and I burned the midnight oil re-organising the routine of the entire establishment to turn out what had become known as 'instant sailors'. The change took place in the summer of 1966 and we only had a term and a half to get settled down before our inspection by the C-in-C and his staff. The staff spent several days examining every department in detail and on the final day the C-in-C, Admiral Sir Varyl Begg, appeared to inspect ceremonial divisions and to walk round the establishment. In the days of the 15 year old boys, the mast was always manned on these occasions with the "Button Boy" standing on the truck. It was assumed that this could no longer be done with 'instant sailors', but the Training Officer found a newly entered class that he thought could do it and so they did, to the delight and admiration of the C-in-C. This helped to produce a highly successful inspection in late November 1966 towards the end of my last term.

On a personal note, I should explain that I was getting near the end of my 6 years time in the promotion zone. During this time, one is reported on every 6 months, the 'flyers' get early promotion to Captain any time after three years seniority, the lesser fry any time up to nine years seniority and the rest get passed over. In such an appointment and after several obviously successful previous appointments, I knew I had a chance of promotion. However the competition was stiff and I had not been getting on with the Captain. He resented me taking compassionate leave while Richard was dying and on several occasions, he had sent for me and complained that I must behave more like a Whale Island officer. Whale Island was the Gunnery school where they taught parade and gun drill with much shouting of order, etc. I had to tell the Captain that as a 'Salt Horse', small Ship Officer, my leadership style was different. The Captain himself, a torpedo specialist, was tall, gangly and highly strung. So also not a Whale Island type. He left at the end of the summer term 1966, and gave me a very complimentary 'flimsy', which is a brief report which is supposed to reflect what he has said in the confidential reports. During the C-in-C's inspection towards the end of the next term, the C-in-C's Chief of Staff, Commodore Brodie Hoare, asked my new Captain (with whom I was getting on very well) what was wrong with his Commander as he had not been recommended for promotion for the previous 18 months? "Nothing wrong at all", said the new Captain, who later told me that it was agreed to make a special effort to get Greenish promoted on one of his last two shots. Alas, no such luck, and in the face of all the competition, I was neither surprised nor disappointed to be 'passed over'. For reasons which will become apparent it was also a blessing in disguise. What I did not like was the fact that my previous Captain had not, as he was supposed to, informed me that he was not recommending me and why. I had experienced the same problem while I was commanding "Termagant", and had sent for the officer and told him. It did him no harm, as he later reached the rank of Commander. During my last term I was informed by my Appointer that I was to go to the Ministry of Defence and asked what department I would like to go to? I had no hesitation in saying that after my experience in both Singapore and the Middle East, I would like to join the newly formed Defence Intelligence Staff (DIS).

CHAPTER 16

BACK TO INTELLIGENCE

IN JANUARY 1967 I joined the DIS and found myself Head of the Indo China Section of D12 which covered the whole of the Far East. Two years earlier, in 1965, the staffs in the Admiralty, War Office and Air Ministry had been combined in one building, the old Air Ministry in Whitehall. In the DIS, those dealing with the Soviet Union remained separate entities, but all other areas were fully integrated. Thus, my Army colleague was Head of the China/Japan section and the Wing Commander looked after South and South East Asia. We each had a mixture of serving and retired officers from all three services but my section was unique, as, dealing with the Vietnam war, I had a US Air Force Lieutenant Colonel and a US West Point Army Captain both on exchange service. I also had a very unique retired Brigadier who had an international reputation as an expert on Indo China. In the past, he had represented the Government in various advisory roles out there and had been allowed to continue serving. He eventually retired at the age of 70! With the family deeply committed in Sussex, a move to London was clearly impractical for my large family, and I settled down to commuting by rail, as I had done previously when serving on the Joint Planning staff. I would reach the office at 08:15 daily or earlier if necessary and leave for home at various times, depending on the work load.

The work entailed reading vast quantities of material from diplomatic sources, the press, GCHQ, MI6 and MI5, and reducing it by analysis to a coherent picture, which at about 09:00 every day, I briefed to the Colonel D12. At 09:30 daily he, in turn, went to the main briefing from all areas to brief the top brass. Occasionally, if the Colonel was not available, we Heads of Sections attended the main briefing. The first hour or so of the day was thus the most hectic, after which one settled down to the other tasks we had. These included the preparation of lectures, articles for intelligence publications and briefing or debriefing diplomats or service officers heading for or arriving back from posts in the Far East. All the time, there was a steady flow of paper into our In trays. Once a year, there was a major conference with our US counterparts in DIA and held alternately in London and Washington. During the four years I was Head of the Indo China Section, I attended this conference in Washington on two occasions and flew to Dulles Airport by RAF VC10 on a Friday, then by local airline to Norfolk, where I spent the weekend with our friends the Faulconers, before returning to Washington on the Sunday evening. The conference would last a week at Arlington Hall with visits to the other agencies including CIA out at Langley, a suburb of Washington.

A further responsibility of the DIS was to contribute our military intelligence to the current political, diplomatic and economic intelligence produced by the other agencies or ministries. This was done by meetings in the Cabinet Officer of 'Current Intelligence Groups' (CIG's) – different groups for different areas. In my time, the Far East CIG was chaired by a Foreign Diplomat, the brilliant Michael Butler, who later rose to become Senior Ambassador. The product of our weekly meeting went to the Joint Intelligence Committee (JIC) chaired by a senior Foreign Office Official and with the Heads of GCHQ, MI6, MI5, and the DIS as members. The approved product was then printed and published in the 'Red Book' which was circulated to the Prime Minister, Senior Ministers, senior Government Officials, Ambassadors etc. Thus the Government was kept abreast of world events from the best and most accurate sources available. I am not going to attempt to recount any details of all this intelligence for two reasons. Firstly, by its nature it was mostly current intelligence reporting ongoing situations week by week. Over my 12 years in the DIS it is impossible to either remember or to describe it all and after all, it is now history. Secondly, I signed the Official Secrets Act whereby I undertook not to disclose any information that I learned in the course of my duties. Before the Falklands war, even the existence of much of the intelligence organisation was unknown to the general public but a great deal of information was released after the Franks Enquiry into intelligence failings before the Argentine invasion.

In the spring of 1968 Alice became ill and had a major operation at St Helen's Hospital in Hastings. At the time, I did not realise just how serious her condition was and the doctors had decided not to tell me. She returned home and resumed a normal life for a while, but months later, was back again in hospital. Early in 1969, my Appointer enquired if I was interested in a final foreign appointment and I explained that this did not look possible. In April 1969 he enquired again for more definite information as I was overdue for relief. That evening I went to see our GP who told me that Alice had a malignant melanoma, that although everything possible had been done, there was never any hope of saving her and that she had not too long to live. All this information had been withheld for the sake of the children and I suppose that I had unconsciously blocked all thought of it out of my mind. So I had to inform all five children by one means or another. Thankfully my elder sister had given up her nursing job and had joined us to look after Alice and the family. Less than a week later on 6th May 1969 Alice died. Naturally, I had compassionate leave over this ghastly period including the funeral and the Appointer delayed any decision about my future. My sister stayed on to look after the family and I soldiered on in the DIS.

Six weeks later I was suddenly summoned by the Vice Chief of Naval Staff (VCNS) and wondered, like a schoolboy, what this was about and what I had done wrong! Only to be told that my name would be in the Queen's birthday honours the next day with the award of an OBE! Unlike civilians who are asked if they are willing to accept an award, it comes as a surprise to service people. My first reaction was bitter disappointment that it had come too late for Alice to know. We had been married for 22 years, during all of which, she had been a wonderful naval wife, accompanying me wherever possible to Malta, Singapore and Canada, and putting up with my numerous absences at sea or Cyprus for example and coping with our growing family on her own. But how did I earn this award? Most Naval Officers know little about ground or air warfare, but the experience I gained in the excellent OTC at Cheltenham College together with the occasional landing party exercise at sea and above all, my abiding interest in modern history, had given me an unusual grasp of land warfare. I knew that the D12 Colonel was happy with the service he was getting about the Vietnam War and interestingly, the naval Commodore (Intelligence) Brodie Hoare was the same man who had been Chief of Staff (COS) at Portsmouth and knew of my bad luck at "St Vincent". I have never seen a citation so can only guess, but on reflection, I realised that it was a very pleasant compensation for the lack of further promotion. At which point, I can also add how fortunate it was that I had not been promoted, as further challenging appointments and moves looked increasingly difficult with a large family and house and no wife. As it was, my Appointer, in due course again asked me what I would like to do and again offered another foreign appointment if I wished. By this time, Simon was at Durham University, Philip about to join him; Vivien, disturbed by all that had happened, was expelled from her Convent School and a problem; Tina and Ben were both about to move school. In these circumstances I took the easy course and asked if I could remain in the DIS and eventually, this was agreed by all concerned. I can only add how grateful I was to the Navy for being such a sympathetic employer. Interestingly both Appointer and the new Commodore (Intelligence) who had arrived had both lost their wives to cancer and so understood my situation better than most.

These memoirs are intended basically to cover my naval career and not the family, but I feel that the events I have just described have had to include the family situation in order to produce a coherent and understandable picture. There is this conflict between career and family and in my day, the Navy generally came first. While I always maintained a high standard of duty, etc, there were times when the family had to be considered. It may have cost me further promotion, who knows, but I have no regrets and indeed, was deeply grateful for the way I was treated, as a senior and soon to be retired Commander.

One of the 'perks' of my intelligence appointment was occasional visits to the parish. During my time as Head of the Indo China section of D12, I flew out by RAF VC10 to Singapore, where we still had a base and then by commercial flights to Indo China. Here, I was able to visit the British Defence Attachés at the embassies in Bangkok, Saigon, Vientiane in Laos and Phnom Penh in Cambodia. In Phnom Penh I stayed in an ancient French Colonial hotel, where I had an enormous room and an even bigger bathroom. This was a memorable visit for another reason too, as a coup took place while I was there. Up till this time, Prince Sihanouk, with left wing sympathies, had managed to keep Cambodia out of the war raging next door in Vietnam, keeping a blind eye on the increasing use of Cambodian territory to ferry supplies down through Laos, down the Ho Chi Minh Trail, to the Viet Cong in the Mekong Delta. This was irritating the South Vietnamese and Americans and led to the coup by General Lon

Nol. Prince Sihanouk fled to Moscow and later Peking, the borders were closed indefinitely and I was stranded! I went to stay with the Defence Attaché and during my enforced stay of nearly two weeks, we travelled out into the country, including an interesting trip to the seaside resort of Ream, near the then new port of Sihanoukville. Here we were the only guests for lunch at a large restaurant on the beach.

The peaceful countryside and people of Cambodia were very attractive and subsequent events including the take over by the brutal Pol Pot regime were tragic. Another British refugee in this situation was the Countess of Brecknock. This majestic lady had taken over the St John's Ambulance organisation after the death of Countess Mountbatten and was on a world tour. She happened to be on a private visit to the famous ruins of Angkor Wat in the north west of the country, when the coup took place and the border closed. In true British fashion she decided to report to her Ambassador, took a taxi and drove some 150 miles to Phnom Penh. One morning days later the Ambassador came into the Defence Attaché's office, turned to me and said that he could not stand the lady any more and I was to take the Embassy Land Rover the following day and escort the Countess to Thailand. How we were to get over the border was apparently left to me and clearly this 200 mile journey was going to be a daunting business. Mercifully, I was saved the trouble as the next morning, following diplomatic pressure, the new government announced two special flights, one to Hong Kong and one to Singapore, on the latter of which, the Embassy got two seats for the Countess and me. On our arrival at Singapore the Countess was met by a large St John's delegation while I slunk away to Changi to beg an RAF flight home!

In about 1971, a well known Army Major General "Noddy" Willison, became Director of Service Intelligence and soon demanded a reorganis-ation of D12 so that we reverted to three single service sections. I thus became head of the naval section covering the whole of the Far East with a staff of two retired Lieutenant Commanders now serving as civilian IOs. But this was by no means a full time task and so I was given responsibility for SEATO with a Squadron Leader as my assistant. This was a huge bonus as he and I flew to Bangkok twice a year to attend the SEATO Intelligence Conferences as the UK representatives. It also gave me the opportunity to visit the Naval SO (I) in Hong Kong and the Naval Attachés or Advisors in Djakarta, Delhi and Islamabad. In D12 the three Heads of Sections now sat in the same office, so I was able to witness my Army colleagues dealing with the disastrous end of the US involvement in the Vietnam War.

Although the retiring age for Commanders was shortly to be extended to 53, I was due to be retired at 50 in October 1972. However earlier that year I was invited to extend my service for a further three years to 53. This I happily agreed to, and continued to serve in D12 until I did eventually retire from the Royal Navy in October 1975.

I had served in the Royal Navy for 35 years, nearly 20 years at sea, including two years in Command, and the rest ashore in many interesting appointments. Intelligence had dominated the latter because it was something I understood and enjoyed. I never had any regrets over the profession and life I had chosen. Like all retiring service personnel, I was invited to attend a course to adapt me to the civilian world. I chose business studies and attended a six week course at the London Polytechnic. This was run by a retired Ghurkha Officer and covered all aspects of business and finance. There was frequent mention of money which he called "The lettuce" but I have to confess that the longer the course ran the more convinced I became that such a life was not for me. At the same time, the civil element of the Defence Intelligence staff telephoned me several times urging me to return to the DIS, as they had an important job they wanted me to do. I had always believed that one should enjoy the job or profession one followed and the salary was a secondary consideration. So it was not a difficult decision and in October 1975 I returned to the DIS as a lowly IO3, as one always had to start from the bottom.

Unfortunately, security clearances which were, of course, in the very highest category for intelligence work, were quite separate for service and civilian personnel. It sounds crazy but I lost my service security clearances on retirement and was given a temporary job while I was vetted for my civilian security clearances. This involved interviews with two referees named by me and examination of my service career and personal affairs. It took six weeks. Not until I received my clearance was I told what this job they wanted me for was to be. I was to join D14 the Middle East Division and was to be the sole desk officer handling the Lebanese Civil War. I had of course been the naval SO(I) Middle East over 15 years earlier and had visited Lebanon, so was familiar with this beautiful little country and some of its complexities. Some years earlier, the Palestinians had pushed their luck in Jordan and after heavy fighting, had been expelled. They were now causing trouble in Southern Lebanon, close to the Israeli border, and where they had local Shia Muslim supporters. But Christians, who occupied most of the mountains of Lebanon and the north, also occupied villages in the south close to the Israeli border. The Christians of Lebanon were divided into at least a dozen different sects, ranging from Maronite Christians to Greek Catholics and each major sect had its own Militia and military leaders. There was also a major Druze faction in central Lebanon with its own Militia. The French, towards the end of their colonial rule, created a constitution in 1943, designed to hold the country together, whereby the President had to be a Maronite Christian, the Prime Minister a Sunni Muslim and the Speaker of the National Assembly a Shia Muslim, and so on down the line. This had worked more or less for over 30 years, but the influx of the Palestinians and their huge refugee camps near Tyre and Sidon and even in Beirut the capital, with all their complex militias had disturbed the status quo and dragged the country into the Arab conflict with Israel. It led to fighting between Christians and Muslims, the loss of control by the Lebanese Government, whose forces became powerless to stop it and eventually the entry of powerful Syrian forces, who wished to seize control of the country. Someone very aptly christened it a proxy Middle East War.

I was pitched into what rapidly became the toughest and most complex situation I had ever had to tackle and I never had to work so hard in my life. I would catch a 6:56 train from home arriving at the office before 8:15, would be immersed in a mass of overnight reports from which I had to prepare a brief and at 9:30, I was on my feet briefing a large roomful of Intelligence top brass. On one occasion, during the Syrian invasion of Lebanon, the Palestinians had destroyed 18 Syrian tanks in the mountain passes to the east of Beirut. When I mentioned this, General Willison said "Rubbish – that's impossible". Afterwards, I had to show him the evidence, which was very clear cut and he had to accept that it was true. Intelligence poured in all day, lunch was a sandwich at the desk and I was seldom home till 8:30pm. This went on for a couple of years but gradually, the pressure eased, the war developed a pattern and by 1978, interest in and influence of this proxy war gradually waned. A welcome relief from the pressure were two visits I was able to pay to the Lebanon. A senior Research Officer and I would fly to Cyprus by RAF transport and then by commercial aircraft to Damascus. Here we would be met by the Defence Attaché, an Army

Lieutenant Colonel who was also accredited to the Lebanon. On the first visit, we drove north through Syria to have a look at Latakia, the Syrian naval base, and then south into Lebanon, visiting Tripoli and through the Christian area to Beirut. On the second visit we crossed into Lebanon near Baalbek and headed as far south as the fighting allowed, also visiting the Druze Headquarters. Then as we headed north to Beirut we caught the attention of a Syrian patrol who arrested us and took us to their Guard Post. Here we were interrogated and I left it to Ian MacKay, the Defence Attaché to use his diplomatic immunity to wriggle us out of this awkward situation and we were soon released and on our way. Beirut by this time was largely in ruins but the Mayflower Hotel where we stayed was fortunately intact.

As the interest in the Lebanese war waned, I became aware of an unexpected vacancy among the Duty Intelligence Officers in the Cabinet Office. I had attempted unsuccessfully once before to become a DIO but this time, after the usual interview and presentation of a CV etc, I was successful. In May 1979 I resigned from my post as an IO2 in DIS and joined the Joint Intelligence Organisation (JIO) across Whitehall in the Cabinet Office. I became one of a team of 5 retired service officers, all with extensive intelligence experience. Two were ex Army, one ex RAF and two ex Royal Navy. Each of us did a 24 hour duty from 11:00 daily and we absorbed all our leave and sickness between us, so that on average, we did a duty every fourth day. In hourly terms, it was equivalent of a normal job and we were paid as such at the rate of a Retired Officer First Class (RO1). The job was to monitor all incoming intelligence from all sources, including the press agencies and to take action to inform the appropriate Ministers and staff when thought necessary. This, of course, was especially important and necessary out of working hours and at weekends and involved considerable judgement when assessing a situation. We were provided with a suite which included a conference room, an office equipped with a range of pigeon holes, a map press, a desk and press agency teleprinters, a bedroom with a TV, a refrigerator and bathroom. A fully manned communications office was just across the passage equipped with online teleprinters from all intelligence agencies and relevant Ministries such as the Foreign Office and MOD. Out of these teleprinters poured a constant stream of intelligence, which we collected as frequently as the situation demanded. If things were quiet, we could usually manage a few hours sleep, but at busy times, one kept going as you could not afford to get behind in coping with the flood of paper. My arrival coincided with the general election and the arrival of Margaret Thatcher as Prime Minister next door at No 10. It quickly became apparent that she would demand the highest standard of service and senior officers had to have a grip on their subject before briefing the Prime Minister. One of our direct telephones was to No 10. So in the event of an incident or important development a call to the duty clerk was de rigeur and contact was often direct with Charles Powell, the PM's Private Secretary for Foreign Affairs when such events occurred. The co-ordinator, Sir Antony Duff who ran the J10 would often appear in the office to enquire if we had informed the PM. It was usually Reuters or Associated Press which produced the first report of an event that would develop into a problem for the UK. There were many minor flaps including, in those days, aircraft hijacks by terrorists. These usually started in the Middle East and we had to watch carefully to see where they were likely to end up. Many of these ended in the UK and eventually an efficient organisation developed whereby we alerted the SAS, the police and those elements that manned the COBRA operations room. The aircraft would be directed to land at Stanstead where their arrival caused the least inconvenience and where the SAS and police would be waiting for them.

During my nine years in the Cabinet Office the biggest crisis without doubt was the Falklands War. There was an intelligence failure partly due to economy of effort towards South America but also because of a conviction that Argentina would not or could not invade. I remember the report of the Argentine scrap metal dealer arriving in South Georgia but he apparently had a contract and its significance was not clear until later it was realised that he was accompanied by troops. Following the invasion of the Falklands Islands and the decision by the Prime Minister to send forces to recover them, the MOD and the Foreign Office immediately went into crisis mode while frantic efforts were made to prepare the fleet and troops for departure on the following Monday. Over the weekend plans developed: I was D10 that Sunday and vividly remember receiving a telephone call that evening from the Secretary of State for Defence requesting the immediate requisition of the liner "Canberra". The Secretary to the Cabinet and his Secretary had gone off on their usual weekend, the Cabinet Office was empty and I had great difficulty in contacting people to get things moving. During the following week, a team led by the Royal Navy Captain from J10 responsible for South America moved into our Conference Room and took over responsibility from us. We kept a watching brief and I recall my naval colleague and I having to teach our army colleagues how to measure distances on a chart as we plotted the fleet moving south.

Time moved on and I neared my 65th birthday and compulsory retirement, but just before, one of my colleagues had to have a heart bypass and was to be away for three months. This was regarded as too long for the D10's to absorb and I was asked to stay on, which I was happy to do. I finally retired in late January 1988 after over 47 years continuous service to the Crown, the Government and above all the Navy. The concept of service, duty and loyalty which dominated my attitude to life is now alas, regarded as old fashioned but I have no regrets at all about the life I chose. I was continually lucky both during the war and afterwards, when I managed to get the appointments I wanted and achieve the destroyer career that had always been my ambition.

I should not end these memoirs without mention of my long and happy retirement. Following remarriage, I sold my house just before I retired and Yvonne and I bought an apartment in the south of France near Antibes. This was expensive both to buy and to maintain, so we let it when not occupying it ourselves. We managed the letting from home which kept me busy, as Yvonne, a doctor, was still working, but it was very successful and led to several friendships with regular clients. After Yvonne followed me into retirement, we spent many happy months down there and, curiously, met up again with Anthony Frodsham, with whom I had served in HMS "Danae" in 1942/43 and who also had an apartment in Antibes. In 2002, on my 80th birthday, I had been led to believe that Yvonne and I were to have dinner "a deux" at our favourite French restaurant. When we got there, to my astonishment, I discovered all of my children and their spouses sitting at the table waiting for us. What a memorable weekend that was!

We have also spent many happy holidays all over the world, including Europe which I hardly knew except for the ports, as well as several cruises. We also have a sizeable garden and I still play golf at my local club. However, more important than all this are our two families who provide us with endless interest and whose achievements are a cause for pride. For several reasons, we have sold our French apartment after nearly 20 years, but still find that we are busy and wonder how on earth we ever found time to work. But keeping active is, I am sure, the key to the long and happy life I have had, as well as having my own personal physician.